"Stefan has a profound grasp of the Industry."

Ron Peltier
CEO, Home Services of America

"The Swanepoel TRENDS Report is the industry's premier report regarding the key factors that are shaping the real estate business. The Report serves as a mirror that we hold up to ourselves to ensure that we're doing the things we need to do to continue to be a highly successful real estate company."

Lennox Scott
CEO, John L. Scott Real Estate, Washington

"Stefan conducts extensive research and truly understands the trends that have and are expected to impact our industry."

Pam O'Connor
CEO, Leading Real Estate Companies of the World

"Stefan is always right on with his trends. The Swanepoel TRENDS Report is a must read."

John P Reinhardt
President, Fillmore Real Estate

"One of the best jobs of 'Pulling It All Together' that I have seen."

Dale Stinton
CEO, National Association of Realtors®

"There is an impressive range of information, literature and publications available to the student of today's real estate industry. However, there is only one place to start the search. The Swanepoel TRENDS Report. It will be found on the desks of industry leaders across the country and will be quoted whenever the decision makers meet."

Jeremy Conaway
President, RECON Intelligence Services

"Stefan's statistics transcend other real estate reports because his research is three-dimensional and gives the user a peek into the future."

Kathy Howe
President-Elect, Real Estate Educators Association

"The Swanepoel TRENDS Report is a tool that every broker and agent must read. It gives you the edge on the competition by knowing what is going to happen rather than saying to yourself after the fact, 'what happened?' In today's changing and volatile market you need to be able to see the future in order to seize your future."

Dirk Zeller
President, Real Estate Champions

"I order, at first opportunity, Stefan's annual publication the Swanepoel TRENDS Report. His work providing the real estate industry timely and valuable information is priceless. I urge Brokers and Agents to take advantage of his keen insights."

Alec Hagerty
Speaker & Trainer, Knowledge Sponge Seminars

"Annually I think it'll be a repeat, but no! Stefan's writings are always fresh, on tempo and full of useable information. Stefan is totally on top of the real estate industry, its actions, reactions, fads, trends and new views."

Jerri Rossi
Author, Dog Eat Dog & Vice Versa

"The Swanepoel TRENDS Report sets a new standard for research on industry trends. I keep a copy on my desk which I utilize often and share with my leadership, members and staff."

Bob Hale
CEO, Houston Association of Realtors®

"For both Brokers and Agents the Swanepoel TRENDS Report provides not only a roadmap but needed guideposts to navigate the real estate profession. Utilizing available resources, the TRENDS Report provides direct recommendations and benchmarks to assist in planning for success in the real estate profession."

Walter Baczkowski
CEO, Metropolitan Consolidated Assn. of Realtors® & Director, Point 2 Technologies

"Stefan cuts through the clutter and the confusion in a sea of change. He skillfully identifies what is truly important to know about our industry heading into 2010 and beyond. The Swanepoel Trends Report is a MUST READ to help us all navigate in the decade ahead."

Ron Seigel
President, Napa Consultants International

TRANSFORMATIONAL CHANGE

SWANEPOEL
TRENDS REPORT
2010

BUSINESS TRENDS IMPACTING
THE REAL ESTATE INDUSTRY

RESIDENTIAL • COMMERCIAL • ECONOMIC • SOCIAL MEDIA

by
Stefan J. M. Swanepoel

Managing Editor:	Thomas M. Mitchell
Research:	Thomas M. Mitchell and Tinus Swanepoel
Editing:	Meredith Blumoff and Steve Hatton
Graphic Design:	Tinus Swanepoel and Laudi Centeno (Cover)

ISBN:	978-0-9704523-2-0

$ 149.95 USA
$ 159.95 CAN
€ 99.95 EUR

Other Publications by the Author:

Real Estate Handbook
A New Era in Real Estate
Swanepoel Top Real Estate Firms
Real Estate Confronts Reality
Real Estate Confronts Technology
Real Estate Confronts the e-Consumer
Real Estate Confronts the Banks
Real Estate Confronts Profitability
Real Estate Confronts Customer Acquisition
The Domino Effect
Real Estate Confronts the Future
Real Estate Confronts Bundled Services
Real Estate Confronts Goal Setting vs. Business Planning
Real Estate Confronts the Information Explosion
Swanepoel TRENDS Report 2006
Swanepoel TRENDS Report 2007
Swanepoel TRENDS Report 2008
Swanepoel TRENDS Report 2009
Swanepoel SOCIAL MEDIA Report 2010

PUBLISHED BY
RealSure Publishing
P O Box 7259
Laguna Niguel, CA 92607

Publisher website:	RealSure.com
Report website:	RETrends.com
Bookstore website:	RealEstateBooks.org

Preface

Although change is an ongoing event — the only constant remaining in life — it doesn't come all at once. Fundamental structural change to a belief system, a political system, a philosophy, a very way of doing business or an industry comes in small, incremental steps that are often too small to notice. But over time those steps pile up and collide with specific events that have a disparate power to cause seismic change and the result is re-engineering on a large scale.

And at this very moment there are many different events indicating that we, as an industry, have found ourselves very close to that nexus.

These major shifts often only occur once or twice in a century or in a person's life. And for us to possibly be at that point in the history of the residential real estate industry is exhilarating.

Please don't resist – embrace.

Please don't wait – move forward.

Please don't criticize – contribute.

Please don't tear down – add value.

Individually and together we can all succeed.

I look forward to "speaking" to all of you during 2010 – in person or online.

Stefan Swanepoel
December 2009

Notice

Confidential Information

No confidential sources were used in this Report and no information identified as confidential under any existing NDA was included without permission from the appropriate authorities. This Report is a result of research, articles that are readily available through the media, websites, social media, reports, notes taken during conventions and seminars and one-on-one discussions with industry leaders.

Involvement

The author may, from time to time serve as a consultant and/or advisor to companies and organizations mentioned in the Report. Specifically he serves as Senior Partner of RealSure, Inc.

Accuracy, Sources and Surveys

As far as possible all statements, statistics and inferences were checked and although great care was undertaken to provide accurate and current information, we cannot accept any responsibility for any liability, loss or risk that may be claimed or incurred as a consequence; directly or indirectly. All sources and publications used to compile this Report are listed in the References section.

RealSure every year consolidates survey data and personal interviews with real estate industry and organizational leaders. Executive interviews were conducted across a nationwide cross-section of over 100 real estate leaders and executives via telephone, email and, as locality allowed, live/in-person meetings. Research and Interviews for this Report were conducted over a 10-month period from March 2009 to December 2009 with the majority during the last three months of the year.

Examples and Disclaimer

References to any companies, products, services and websites do not constitute or imply endorsement and neither is any reference or absence of reference intended to harm, place at a disadvantage or in any other way affect any company or person. Information contained in this Report should not be a substitute for common sense, thorough research and competent advice. Readers are urged to consult proper counsel or other authority regarding any points of law, finance, technology and business before proceeding and all conclusions expressed herein are subject to local, state and federal laws and regulations.

Trademarks

Most of the companies listed in this Report own numerous trademarks and it has not been possible to identify each respective trademark. Specifically Realtor® is a registered trademark of the National Association of Realtors®. This Report does not in any way seek to challenge or dilute any of these marks.

Table Of Contents

Book 1

2009 in Review

TRENDSETTERS

of the

YEAR 2009

TRENDSETTERS are those Companies that during the year set forth actions that were different and memorable that could have far reaching impact on the real estate industry in the years to come.

We salute you and thank you for your contribution toward making our industry a better place.

#10 Redfin

Launched in February 2006, Redfin is an interesting hybrid of a real estate company that, despite the last three difficult years, has been able to survive and expand. The company bills itself as an online real estate brokerage company providing a combination of employee agents and online real estate search. Redfin has one of the best websites in the real estate space and has often been the first to implement innovations such as IDX, AVMs, etc. Redfin reimburses roughly half of the buy-side real estate fee directly upon closing. It is also one of the lowest cost models in the industry today and is clearly a future model worth watching very closely.

#9 Metro Brokers

Metro Brokers was started with one office and a handful of sales associates in 1979 and in 2009 it was the world's largest GMAC Real Estate franchise. Under the leadership of Kevin Levent, who became president and CEO in 1996, the company has grown to nearly 2,000 sales associates. It is, however, its departure as a franchise from GMAC under a legal cloud of disagreement and the move across in December 2009 to the newly re-launched and still relatively small national franchise Better Homes & Gardens (BH&G) that makes Kevin one of the top 10 Newsmakers of the Year. Not only is this the largest franchisee switch ever but, ironically, Metro Brokers actually was a BH&G franchise two decades back before BH&G decided to exit from the residential real estate brokerage business.

#8 HomeServices of America

HomeServices may be the nation's second-largest full-service independent residential real estate brokerage firm, but that's not why we have decided to include it. It's just that almost every time a crown jewel in real estate changes hands you can place a bet that HomeServices is on the receiving side. In September 2009 Koenig & Strey GMAC, as a result of the GMAC franchise acquisition by Canada-based Brookfield RPS, became available. Founded in 1961 Koenig & Strey has approximately 900 agents throughout 21 offices serving Chicago, the North Shore, Lake County and the western suburbs and was one of the leaders in Chicago with sales in 2008 of $2.6 billion. No points for guessing who snagged this great company. It was the 21st such key acquisition for HomeServices, which now has more than 15,000 real estate professionals. Well done, Ron Peltier and Warren Buffet.

Google

Many were surprised when we listed Google as a Newsmaker two years ago, and subsequently, many have thought that although it's a dynamic company, it is first and foremost a search engine and would never really go anywhere from there as a business. But I just don't see it that way. We have always loved Google and continue to feel that they are and will for a long time to come continue to be the single biggest outside driver on our industry. Remember the Google Maps API, Google Adwords, Google Mail, Google Apps, Street View and Google Chrome? The list goes on. Many of these initiatives have value and potential for the real estate industry. Brian Boero of 1000Watt Consulting brought to our attention only recently Google's move to include a real estate overlay on Google Maps, which puts listings smack-dab in front of millions of Google users. It is very likely that few in the industry had any idea that the company spent the last several years quietly aggregating this content. Furthermore, Google also includes a unique page for every listing that incorporates photos, a map (including Street View), property details, directions, transit information and more: basically a listing detail page. And this is not the end as there are hundreds of additional ways Google will still advance real estate innovation, directly and indirectly.

@properties

In one of the hardest hit regions of the country Chicago real estate firm @properties is not only surviving, it's thriving. The company, which was established just 10 years ago as a boutique sales and marketing operation serving developers of new-construction condos, has grown into a mega brokerage. This year more than 200 experienced agents joined the company, catapulting it to the number-one spot in market share in Chicago. With more than $1.5 billion in annual sales and 800 agents the company enjoys a 95% agent-retention rate and a much sought after image and market awareness.

RE/MAX International

RE/MAX led the way in being the first national real estate company to aggregate and post all homes for sale, whether theirs or that of a competitor, on their website, remax.com. This was generally frowned upon by many in the industry and most large national franchises did not follow. As a matter of fact, companies such as Coldwell Banker and Century 21 in the Realogy stable went exactly the opposite way by posting only their listings. Then RE/MAX built a top 10 real estate website based on consumer traffic. Yes, the rankings fluctuated depending which rating and ranking system you used — or which month — but overall RE/MAX out ranked the three largest franchises (Century 21, Coldwell Banker and Keller Williams) consistently and comfortably. Unquestionably the extensive media and TV campaigns helped, but overall remax.com offered the consumer a better experience than any of the others. Well done.

Brookfield Residential Property Services

Barely a year ago the real estate industry was stunned when Canada-based Brookfield RPS, a division of Brookfield Asset Management, Inc. (Brookfield) and owner of Royal LePage, one of the top two residential real estate franchises in Canada, acquired GMAC Real Estate. Then, in November 2009, the company announced its second major move when it acquired the Real Living Network Services, a subsidiary of Real Living Inc. By combining the two companies Brookfield has created one of America's leading residential real estate franchises with more than $20 billion in annual home sales and an estimated 30,000 agents. Many of the GMAC franchises in the U.S. are expected to convert to the Real Living brand in 2010, and with an estimated 10,000 agents it will rank them close to the 10th largest in the U.S. based on agent count.

Lending Processing Services

Lending Processing Services (LPS) became a newly independent and publicly traded company as a result of Fidelity Information Services spin off in 2008. That makes LPS the industry's number-one provider of mortgage processing services, settlement services and default solutions along with being the nation's leading provider of integrated data, servicing and technology solutions for mortgage lenders. In 2009 FNRES, including Cyberhomes, became a division of LPS and LPS is the company with whom the NAR signed a 10-year agreement to create the RPR (Realtors® Property Resource) and provide the data analytics for the RVM (Realtor® Valuation Model). These are two major projects that could very well shape the way real estate data is sourced in the future.

National Association of Realtors®

For the NAR, 2009 was not an average year. The Realtors® Federal Credit Union started its first full year in operation and with 3,000 members it's already larger than 60% of all credit unions in the U.S. The Realtor® Property Resource (RPR) is considered to be the ultimate member benefit, as well as an attempt to create the largest single source of real estate information in the world. HouseLogic was launched as a free source of information and tools for consumers with the stated goal of becoming one of the top 10 real estate websites. Game Changers was set in motion whereby 14 state and local associations are beta testing 14 different concepts and projects to reinvent the Realtor® association from the inside out. And then there is the Second Century Venture Fund that was formed and funded to acquire strategic equity stakes in key and important technology initiatives, the first of which — DocuSign — has already been made. Very impressive indeed.

The
TRENDSETTER
of the
YEAR 2009

Keller Williams International

Last year's inclusion of Keller Williams International as one of the top 10 Trendsetters was validated when Steve Murray announced in his REAL Trends survey in March that the company had surpassed RE/MAX to become the third largest real estate company in the country based on agent count. This accomplishment marks the first newcomer to the "Top 3" in two decades. This was followed by receiving the highest overall satisfaction rating by J.D. Powers & Associates. Then, in December 2009, Entrepreneur Magazine ranked Keller Williams as the #1 real estate franchise and our own survey of over 10,000 agents ranked Keller Williams as the most recognized real estate franchise brand as voted by the industry. In 2009 Keller Williams, against the general trend, out-performed other major franchises by adding more agents during a tough real estate recession than any other. Well done, Keller Williams International. You are the current crown prince of the Real Estate Brokerage Industry.

#1

NEWSMAKERS

of the

YEAR 2009

NEWSMAKERS are those People that, during the year made headlines as individuals or as a result of the actions and leadership of Companies or Associations they are involved with. Newsmakers are more about the People than the Companies. Companies are featured under Trendsetters.

We salute you and thank you for your contribution toward making our industry a better place.

John Bearden

As one of the most beloved executives of a national franchise, John's sudden departure this year as President of GMAC Real Estate — shortly after the sale of the company to Canada-based Brookfield Residential Property Services — came somewhat as a surprise. Not because he has cited health reasons, but because his departure was rumored to be unpleasant. This after he had been largely responsible for salvaging the sinking franchise during difficult times when former parent General Motors Acceptance Corporation was less than excited about their subsidiary and much more concerned about their own mortgage woes. John, you did an outstanding job under difficult circumstances and we have no doubt that you will once again serve the Industry in another important capacity. We salute you.

Marc Davison and Brian Boero

Outside the box — way outside the box. If ever there was an "odd couple" in real estate these two are it. But just like Jack Lemmon and Walter Matthau these two are top notch in what they do and have created an exciting and dynamic consulting and speaking practice. Marc has an extensive career in advertising with companies like Young and Rubicam while Brian served for many years as President of Inman News. They both worked together at a company they owned called VREO, Inc. before joining forces again to create 1000Watt Consulting. Today they are contributing to the re-engineering of the real estate industry through their consulting engagements.

Kevin Levent

Metro Brokers was started with one office and a handful of sales associates in 1979 and by 2009 it was the world's largest GMAC Real Estate franchise. Under the leadership of Kevin Levent, who became President and CEO in 1996, the company has grown to nearly 2,000 sales associates. It is, however, its departure as a franchise from GMAC under a legal cloud of disagreement and the move across in December 2009 to the newly re-launched and still relatively small national franchise Better Homes & Gardens that makes Kevin one of the top 10 Newsmakers of the Year.

Harley E. Rouda, Jr.

Many where surprised when we listed Harley and his wife Kaira as top 10 Newsmakers for the year 2007, but it had then and has now again proven to be accurate. Since then this couple has skillfully positioned and branded their regional real estate company — Real Living — to be the ideal acquisition company. In October 2009 that is exactly what happened when Canada-based Brookfield Residential Property Services acquired Real Living, converted its GMAC franchise to the Real Living brand and appointed Harley as the new President of the franchise division, which is estimated to have approximately 10,000 agents in the U.S. as a result of the merger and conversion.

Sherry Chris

She may not be CEO of one of the country's largest real estate franchises (yet), but Sherry is unquestionably the most visible one in the media. She is extremely active in the Social Media world of Facebook and Twitter and in attendance at an astounding number of real estate conventions and events. After skillfully climbing the ladder from Royal LePage to Real Living, to Prudential California and then to Coldwell Banker, her accession as CEO of the relatively new re-launched Better Homes & Gardens franchise is nothing short of amazing.

 ### David Stevens

In late September 2009 the Federal Housing Administration (FHA) announced that it had hired David Stevens, a former executive with Wells Fargo, Freddie Mac and Long & Foster as its first Chief Risk Officer. The FHA has not seen a technology upgrade or any staff increases in a decade and the appointment of a Chief Risk Officer is the first in its 74-year history. David has already taken steps to shore up the agency's credit position. The future is promising.

 ### Dale Ross & Marty Frame

Dale and Marty are the two drivers that, over an 11-month period, cobbled together the highest profile merger of the year, one in which the National Association of Realtors® acquired ownership to a copy of the source code of Cyberhomes. This merger, together with a long-term agreement with LPS to provide extensive tax data, hosting and data aggregation services, makes it possible to form the core of RPR (The Realtor® Property Resource) a key part of the NAR's Second Century Initiatives.

 ### Andy Kaufman

Andy Kaufman, a Keller Williams agent in Berkeley, California and a regular AgentGenius.com writer, is credited for founding RE BarCamp. Started in August 2008 to coincide with Inman Connect, RE BarCamp events have exploded in popularity. This unconvention is an ad-hoc gathering of people (real estate professionals from different facets of the business) to share and learn in an open environment. It is a dynamic and intense event with discussions, demonstrations and interaction between the attendees. In 2009 RE BarCamps were held in 20 major cities across the country with one held in San Diego just before the NAR 2009 Convention that pulled in over 500 participants.

 ### Richard A. Smith

Richard is best known as the president and chief executive officer of Realogy Corporation, a global provider of real estate and relocation services and the parent company for real estate franchise brands such as Coldwell Banker, Century 21, ERA Real Estate, Sotheby's International Real Estate and Better Homes & Gardens Real Estate. However, in 2009 it was not well known that Richard tirelessly campaigned and lobbied in Washington to get the first-time homebuyer's tax credit extended to April 2010. It was an extension that also included a $6,500 credit for qualified repeat homebuyers. Well done Richard, the industry thanks you for a job well done.

The
NEWSMAKER
of the
YEAR 2009

Dale Stinton

Just three years into office and Dale has pulled the trigger to move forward on more bold and innovative projects than have been initiated in the previous 10 years combined. Many of his Second Century Initiatives were launched in 2009 and several are so large that they could individually have a significant and long-term impact on the entire residential real estate brokerage industry. The Realtors® Federal Credit Union started its first full year in operation and the Realtors® Property Resource, together with HouseLogic, was announced days before the annual National Association of Realtors® Convention in November. These are huge steps for the NAR and the industry.

#1

EVENTS

of the

YEAR 2009

EVENTS are those occurrences that transpired during the previous calendar year that made headlines, captured the industry's attention and imagination and became the biggest discussion topics of the year. The selections were also based upon their projected future impact on the industry, rather than solely on their performance in 2009.

Houston Becomes #1 REALTOR® Association

In August 2009 the Houston Association of Realtors® (HAR) officially became the largest local Realtor® board in the United States following a recent rise in their membership and a decline in membership at the Long Island (New York) Board of Realtors® (LIBOR). HAR, with a membership of 23,354, surpassed its long standing rival for the top slot by 118. These two have long been the largest local associations by far with the Greater Las Vegas Association of Realtors® holding the third spot with nearly 10,000 fewer members. Congratulations to Bob Hale and his team.

Metro Brokers Switches Franchise Brands

With 2,000 sales associates, the brand switch Metro Brokers made in December 2009 from GMAC to Better Homes & Gardens recorded the largest move of one brokerage company from one franchise brand to another. The departure away from the number-one GMAC franchise in the world to become the number-one BH&G franchise in the world was a major move and strongly refutes the high value many franchises have attached to their brands. Many observe this move as the beginning of more swaps to come as franchisees increasingly look for more than just a name. They want visionary leadership, quality training, technology, Internet and Social Media savvy solutions and, above all, a dependable partner.

RE BarCamp Sets Event Benchmark

RE BarCamp is an ad-hoc gathering of people (real estate professionals from different facets of the business) that share and learn in an open environment. It is widely referred to as an unconvention, with no pre-determined programs or invited guest speakers delivering PowerPoint presentations from a stage. Rather, the structure follows a roundtable of open discussion concerning topics sourced from the registrants and as a result of interaction between attendees. It may only have started in August 2008, but in 2009 it exploded to over 20 major cities across the country and is currently one of the "happening" events in real estate.

RVMs & AVMs Become Strategic

AVM (Automated Valuation Model) is the term widely used to describe the process of providing property valuation by using a mathematical algorithm based on the data. In real estate, AVMs calculate the value of a specific property by analyzing the value of comparable properties sold and registered. The newly announced RVM (Realtor® Valuation Model) utilizes the same mathematical analysis but hopes to aggregate the information available from 700+ MLSs (Multiple Listing Service) across the country. The NAR, the driver behind the RVM, hopes that this model will become the default valuation method for all financial institutions nationwide. If achieved this will be a major industry game changer.

Realtor® Credit Union Celebrates First Year of Operation

One year ago at the 2008 Realtors® Conference & Expo in Orlando, the NAR announced that it had received regulatory approval and a charter for Realtors® Federal Credit Union (RFCU). The Rockville, Maryland-based credit union works in partnership with the NAR as a Realtor® Benefits Program Partner, but it operates totally separate from the NAR with its own board of directors and management team. Now, one year later, RFCU has 3,000 members, $25 million in assets, $16 million in deposits and $8 million in loans, making it larger than 60% of all credit unions today. Impressive. With a stated goal of being in the top 5% of all credit unions within five years the RFCU is definitely a sleeping giant.

Keller Williams Climbs to Third Largest Real Estate Franchise

In March Keller Williams Realty Inc. announced at its 2009 annual convention that it had moved ahead of RE/MAX International to now claim the third-largest real estate franchise in the U.S. with 72,794 associates at the end of 2008 according to a study by Steve Murray of REAL Trends. According to Keller Williams, the growth gained momentum during the last three years of the downturn, where it outpaced most other real estate franchises that had lost agents. During the period from 2006 to 2008 KW increased its associate count by an astonishing 52%. Watch out Century 21 and Coldwell Banker, you have someone coming up fast in your rear view mirror.

Short Sales and Foreclosures Maintain High Visibility

After increasing more than 30% per year for the last four years, some estimate that foreclosures will drop to about 1.75 million in 2010/11. The Treasury Department continues to place pressure on mortgage lenders to make trial loan modifications permanent. Furthermore, in December the Treasury set long-awaited guidelines designed to simplify and speed up the short-sale process through its Home Affordable Foreclosure Alternatives Program. Until now the short-sale process has been cumbersome for all involved, taking as long as eight to 10-months to close a transaction. The program goes into effect April 5, 2010.

Brookfield RPS Acquires a Great Solution

Announcing their second largest acquisition in November 2009, Brookfield RPS became the owner of Real Living Network Services. Combining all the residential real estate brokerage companies Brookfield now owns in Canada and the U.S., makes them one of North America's top 10 leading residential real estate franchises, with more than $20 billion in annual home sales and an estimated 30,000 agents. The reason the Ohio-based Real Living acquisition is such a great solution for Brookfield is that the GMAC franchise they acquired last year was lacking momentum, a CEO and contractually had to replace their name. This acquisition provided them a solution for all three challenges with very little duplication. Congrats Graham Badan.

RPR Becomes the NAR Convention Buzz

Squeezing in a botched (who was invited and who wasn't) and a confusing (intermingling a B2B and B2C initiative) talking head video press announcement a week before the NAR convention was surprising. However, the timing was great as the buzz propelled the Realtors® Property Resource (RPR) into the most discussed and debated topic at the convention. Although billed as the largest single source of real estate information in the world and the "ultimate" member benefit it is also ridiculed as a threat to MLSs across the country. One thing is certain, it is the most significant project undertaken by the NAR in years.

The
EVENT
of the
YEAR 2009

Extended Tax Credit Helps Boost Housing Market

In the hopes of sustaining the real estate market's recent momentum President Obama signed the Worker, Homeownership and Business Assistance Act of 2009 in November, extending the FTHBC until April 2010. The legislation includes language that significantly expands the popular first-time homebuyer tax credit to more than two-thirds of current homeowners and nearly all first-time buyers. On its own this will not save the housing market, but it sparked a rush to buy homes before the extension was approved in November. This resulted in an increase of 7.4% over October for a record 545,000 housing units sold. With rising unemployment and a sluggish economic recovery let's hope that the incentive created by the tax credit carries the housing market through to the summer of 2010.

#1

Overview of Key Market Segments

- Economic Overview
- Commerical Overview
- Social Media Overview

Residential Economics

Potholes and Speed Bumps

INTRODUCTION

It seems like it all started one morning when Wall Street woke up and realized they really didn't have anything to sell their best customers: China and India. So they sat down and packaged up some new products: Collateralized Loan Obligations, Commercial Backed Mortgage Securities and Residential Backed Mortgage Securities. A great idea but as Richard Bove, a financial strategist with Rochdale Securities, noted: "They had a problem — where to find someplace to generate $2 trillion worth of product."

The obvious market was real estate but the boom was rolling along with a shrinking population. But not to worry, Wall Street just pushed deeper into the market. They got buyers qualified with the help of the government and a plethora of home-baked mortgages — Interest Only, Negative Amortization and of course all those Subprime Mortgages — all of which grew debt three times faster than income. The lack of control in the sector resulted in excessive lending and often an absence of credit checks that brought about the only possible outcome; a total collapse of the economy. Then we watched as the federal government rushed in and began doing what only it can do: throw obscene amounts of money at the crisis.

And so we watched it all unfold as we moved deeper and deeper into the current recession with unemployment at its highest level in years — 10.2% to 17% depending on who is included — and a real estate market trying to dig itself out of a very cold snow drift. Just how much snow has been shoveled to date is a matter of opinion and there certainly isn't a shortage of those. Opinions are being offered from every corner and they range from overly positive to extremely negative. Every side of the issue has been hashed out by the experts for months and every conclusion has been supported by one theory or another.

This overview will sort through some of the opinions presented by all major sides of the issue to obtain a better understanding of where we are. And in order

FLASH BACK

"The prices of houses seem to have reached a plateau, and there is reasonable expectancy that prices will decline."
Time Magazine, 1947

"Houses cost too much for the mass market. Today's average price is around $8,000 - out of the reach for two-thirds of all buyers."
Science Digest, 1948

"The goal of owning a home seems to be getting beyond the reach of more and more Americans. The typical new house today costs about $28,000."
BusinessWeek, 1969

"You might well be suspicious of 'common wisdom' that tells you, 'Don't wait, buy now... Continuing inflation will force home prices and rents higher and higher.'"
NEA Journal, 1970

"The median price of a home today is approaching $50,000... Housing experts predict price rises in the future won't be that great."
Nations Business, 1977

"The era of easy profits in real estate may be drawing to a close."
Money Magazine, 1981

"The golden-age of risk-free run-ups in home prices is gone."
Money Magazine, 1985

"Most economists agree.... [a home] will become little more than a roof and a tax deduction, certainly not the lucrative investment it was through much of the 1980s."
Money Magazine, 1986

"Financial planners agree that houses will continue to be a poor investment."
Kiplinger's Personal Financial Magazine, 1993

"A home is where the bad investment is."
San Francisco Examiner, 1996

to do that we first need to take a snapshot of where we find ourselves at the dawn of this new decade.

THERE IS A LOT ON THE TABLE

The rest of the world has found a way to rebound faster from the global recession than the U.S., a recession that has been hanging around since December 2007.

As we sit down at the table today we are faced with an economy that is struggling to find a way out in the midst of a bunch of aggressive government bailouts that have been propping up the market that at the same time are utilizing taxpayer dollars to restock the corporate bank accounts: those of Wall Street companies, financial institutions, insurance companies and automobile companies.

We endured four consecutive quarters of negative GDP until our economy finally grew by 2.2% in the third quarter of 2009. But while we may be moving in the right direction, there are many challenges in front of us that won't make the road to recovery an easy or fast one: Here are two examples of the many potholes that will need to be worked around.

The Stimulus

There was remarkably little stimulus in the stimulus instituted by the government last February; it was more about transfer payments and government outlays. It appears to be wearing off sooner than

expected. It appears that it was too little too late to stem the rising rate of unemployment. In the construction industry for example, the Associated General Contractors of America (agc.org) has reported that 44% of contractors are expected to lay off more workers due to the economic conditions. This will have a significant impact on the states as they suffer from falling tax revenues that continue to drive deeper and deeper budget cuts. The same survey also showed that 76% of contractors expect state transportation departments to put less work out to bid in 2010 than they did in 2009.

Over the next 12 to 18 months the country is going to be challenged with finding ways to reduce the estimated deficits that average over $1 trillion per year for the next eight years. Continued federal spending hasn't worked so far and banks are still failing at an incredible rate: 140 had closed in 2009 at the time of writing this Report (more banks than in 1992 at the height of the savings and loan crisis).

And Americans find themselves caught in the vortex, looking for a way out.

Foreclosures

Along the road to 2010 the Federal Reserve (federalreserve.gov) has been pumping hundreds of billions into the credit markets to hold mortgage rates down. This has not had a major impact on the number of foreclosures. Lower rates are less important in saving homes than not having a job and household income. According to RealtyTrac (realtytrac.com), the total number of foreclosures for 2009 is expected to exceed 3.5 million. A New York Times Poll released in December reported that 26% of unemployed Americans have been threatened with eviction or foreclosure and 13% have lost their homes; 86% are in a financial crisis due to loss of employment. As 2009 came to a close we began to see a rise in the default rate among prime mortgages, which have been viewed as immune to the high defaults hitting subprime loans. According to Moody's Economy.com (economy.com), the number of foreclosures will increase in 2010 to about 4.6

Asia at the Close of 2009

China's economic growth engine has reaccelerated.

Japan has returned to modest growth.

million, of which only an estimated 1.9 million will be sold. Clearly we are going to see the banks holding more property — and that poses a big problem.

This may be more of a problem as certain banks are even holding certain foreclosed and distressed properties off the market, hoping to be able to sell them when the economy becomes stronger. This "Shadow Inventory," according to First American Corelogic (facorelogic.com), is estimated to be as much as 1.7 million homes. So just how many loans are in arrears or have been foreclosed upon and not listed on the market is anyone's guess at this point.

According to Fitch Ratings (fitchratings. com), 2010 will see 88% of the $189 billion in outstanding option ARMs coming up for recasting; 94% have only been making interest-only payments. The fact that interest rates have remained low will be of some relief, but if the Fed raises interest rates the problem will grow. In addition, as house prices have been falling, most of the ARMs will not be able to be refinanced without borrowers putting more cash into the property.

That will be problematic at best if the current level of unemployment continues, very problematic for the real estate market.

REAL ESTATE – TWO VIEWS

2009 was certainly a year of mixed reviews for the housing market. Experts on both sides made predictions throughout the year, some of which were valid and others that fell by the wayside. In many cases their opinions were a mixed bag with both good news and bad. All in all, they have reaffirmed that where we are at the beginning of the next decade is still undecided.

View I – The Worst Is Behind Us

There are many experts that believe that the three-year housing drop finally bottomed out at the end of 2009 and that it will begin to stabilize. With the bargain hunters entering the market the long road back may actually be here. The absence of easy credit in an economy that will continue to be weak in 2010 making that road a tough one. However, the experts feel that at least the downward spiral seems to have abated. One of the leading proponents of that position is the NAR.

> **"** As investors, we all know that the U.S. housing market will eventually rebound. Consumer interest in housing will be fueled by improving business conditions, renewed jobs growth, a loosening of credit restraints for mortgages and the demands of a growing population for new and better places to live. **"**

LARRY D. SPEARS
Contributor, moneymorning.com

As Seen By the NAR

According to a study by Real Estate Economy Watch (realestateeconomywatch.com), the National Association of Realtors® (NAR; realtor.org), the National Association of Homebuilders (NAHB; nahb.org), the Mortgage Bankers Association (MBA; mbaa.org), Fannie Mae (fanniemae.com) and Freddie Mac (freddiemac.com), the recession is behind us. They are all predicting solid growth in 2010, with home sales increasing by 9.6%, reaching an estimated 5.4 million units.

The NAR began seeing a glimmer of hope in the latter part of 2009. Their confidence index toward the end of the year indicated that the home sales outlook had improved significantly toward "moderate confidence" for the single family market, which was up from the lows experienced earlier in the year.

In his comments in December, NAR's Chief Economist Dr. Lawrence Yun pointed to the fact that many buyers were rushing to take advantage of the FTHBC before it was extended to April 30, 2010. He believes that there is still a large, pent-up demand that can be tapped before the credit expires, which will show up as another surge in the spring and early summer. In the area of fundamentals Yun indicted that with the abnormal drop in home prices over the past few years, the price-to-income ratio has fallen below the historic trend line and the overcorrection needs to be halted. At the same time this is adding to the buying power of the typical family, with affordability conditions at the highest on record dating back to 1970. He cautions, though, that prices are beginning to flatten and are poised to rise next year.

> 66 The recession is behind us but the effects of it will linger for some time in the form of higher unemployment and lower levels of business investment and home construction 99
>
> **JAY BRINKMANN**
> Chief Economist, Mortgage Bankers Association

In his presentation in Atlantic City in December 2009 Yun revealed his research that supports the NAR's outlook for 2010. Here are several of the key issues for 2010 through the eyes of the NAR:

- The housing stimulus (FTHBC and higher loan limits) will boost existing home sales in 2010 by 15% with an accompanying boost in home prices of 3% to 5%.

- The Housing Affordability Index is at an all-time high (160) going into 2010; the previous high water mark was 155 in 1972.

- America adds three million more people each year and forms between 1.0 to 1.4 million households. If 300,000 demolitions are taken into account, 2010 will need 1.0 to 1.7 million new units. Housing starts in 2010 will be too little too late.

- Foreclosure inventory will continue to rise in 2010 but will get cleared off quickly.

- The overall economic outlook with the exception of unemployment will improve:

FORECLOSURE INVENTORY

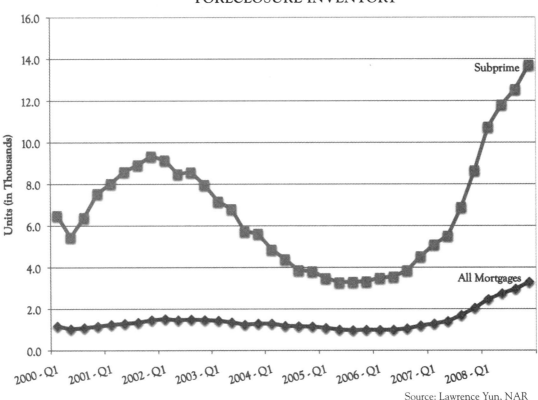

Source: Lawrence Yun, NAR

- GDP will once again turn positive at 2.6%; the 50-year average is 3.3%.

- CPI inflation will increase to 1.6% but remain well below the 50-year average of 4.1%.

inflationary pressure in the economy the association is anticipating an improving market in 2010.

However, as we shall see a bit later, even the NAR has its concerns.

> " Year over year declines in home process by virtually every measure are now moving back toward zero, and we expect most measures of home pricing to move back into positive territory, in comparison with prior-prices, in next Spring's home buying season, which could fuel renewed speculative interest in this beleaguered market. "

DR. MICHAEL ENGLUND
Chief Economist, Action Economics

- Unemployment will remain high at 10%, well above the 50-year average of 5.9%.

- The overall housing forecast for 2010 looks brighter than it did at this time last year.

- Existing home sales will reach 5.7 million units.

- New home sales will hit 560,000, well below the needed number.

- Home price growth will reach 4%.

So from the NAR's perspective, the increases in personal income and consumer spending that occurred in the fourth quarter of 2009, along with the rising confidence index, point to a turnaround in the market. With new home sales showing the initial signs of stabilization and almost no

View II – We May Be Turning the Corner

We also took the market's pulse from a number of other experts that closely watch the real estate industry from the outside and have a more cautious view.

- CNBC's (cnbc.com) real estate correspondent Diana Olick followed suit with her prediction that the housing market will recover in the latter half of the year after dipping in early 2010 when the plug is pulled on the First-Time Homebuyer's Credit (FTHBC; see Trend #2) and the Fed's Fannie Mae and Freddie Mac mortgage purchase programs.

HOUSING STARTS: TOO LITTLE TOO LATE

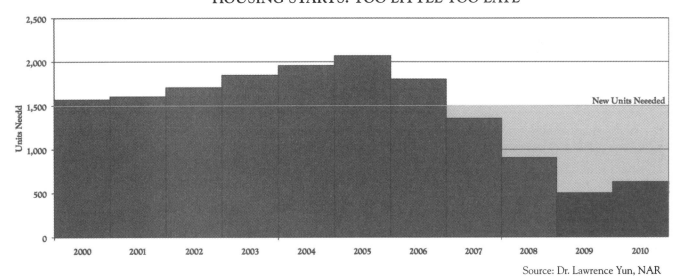

Source: Dr. Lawrence Yun, NAR

- Chief Economist for Action Economics (actioneconomics.com), Dr. Michael Englund, notes that the one "big bright spot" for the U.S. economy in 2010 will be the same thing that was its Achilles Heel over the last three years: the housing market. He believes that the sharp rebound in pending and existing home sales in 2009 placed a floor under U.S. housing starts and other early indicators of home building activity and has allowed some recovery in new home sales.

>  Fewer foreclosure filings sure seems like good news, but lender actions against borrowers have stalled, not ended. Foreclosure activity is being delayed, deferred and put on hold with foreclosure moratoriums, legal challenges and loan modification efforts. 𝟐𝟐

PETER G. MILLER
Syndicated Columnist, OurBroker.com

- Former NAR Chief Economist Dr. David Lereah sees 2010 as a year of modest improvement with mortgage rates hovering between 5.0 and 5.25% as a result of the Fed and modest inflationary pressures. He noted that while there are still some problems ahead (covered in the next section), the fact that in October home sales were up, inventories were down and values were stabilizing was a good sign.

- Credit Suisse Group (credit-suisse.com) anticipates recovery in the housing market based upon the early stabilization achieved in the latter part of 2009. They base their beliefs on the decline in the rate of foreclosures, record high affordability levels and the FTHBC. They believe the housing market has achieved a "tentative sense of balance" with a narrow path that could lead to a modest upside versus significant downside risk if conditions deviate from this path.

All in all, those who view the glass as half-full generally took the third and fourth quarter results as an indicator of an improved market for 2010. While no one is standing on a soapbox and shouting that the worst is over, there is at least a growing sentiment toward finding a light at the end of the tunnel. But then there are the experts that aren't so sure that light is in fact daylight.

CONCERNS THAT LIE AHEAD

But there also appears to be some very serious concerns among many of the experts regarding where the real estate market will find itself in 2010. These concerns focus on several specific issues that we have outlined below.

Let's first take a look at one that, while they see encouraging signs (noted above), they have some serious concerns.

While Lawrence Yun of the NAR has a positive outlook overall he also raises several areas of concern including:

- Foreclosures in 2010 will be just as high in 2009 with distressed sales remaining at roughly 30% of the market.

- Exceptional sales in November drove inventory down but 2010 could see levels increase back to eight months or higher.

- All cash purchases in 2009 reached 19%, double normal levels.

- The FTHBC should be viewed as a lowering of the price and therefore a real decline in value resulting in a further destruction of wealth (see Trend #2).

- The impact that the impending debacle in the commercial real estate market will have on the residential market; poised to take place in 2010 (see Special Overview in Commercial Real Estate).

Here are concerns of others to watch the real estate

market closely:

- Although he views 2010 as a year of modest improvement, Dr. David Lereah is also concerned that the market is still very fragile and vulnerable to a pull-back in government subsidies (see Trend #2) and/or an onslaught of foreclosures. He sees the housing industry as being propped up by a maze of federal programs, direct subsidies, lenient government underwriting practices and an enormous mortgage-backed security purchase program. When combined with the backlog of foreclosures due to hit the street next year the result is a tenuous picture of the housing situation. The removal of the FTHBC and the Federal Reserve's security purchase programs pose a serious threat to the market's recovery next year.

- Janice Revell of Money Magazine (money.cnn.com) sees housing as beginning to stabilize but is concerned that pressure from mounting foreclosures and tight credit will follow the market into 2010. One of the key concerns regarding whether or not the Fed will continue its efforts to keep short-term interest rates low and get credit flowing. If deficit fears among bond investors lead to a sharp rise in long-term Treasury yields, then she points out that housing will suffer, since mortgage rates generally move with 10-year treasuries.

- Dr. David Crowe, Chief Economist at NAHB (nahb.org), expects a little stall in 2010. NAHB predicts annualized sales averaging 5.5 million for the year, with a more starts early in the year and fewer later. Crowe noted that the economy and the job market didn't pick up as was predicted in 2009 and, as a consequence, is rolling into 2010.

- The American Bankers Association's Economic Advisory Committee (aba.com) sees more affordable home prices and low interest rates helping the housing market hit bottom but not until home prices fall another 5% to 10%, sometime in 2010. This won't be eased by an unemployment rate that will remain high for some time, not getting below 9.5% at any point in 2010. And an unemployment rate above 9% presents a problem to the housing market.

- Dr. Mark Zandi, Chief Economist of Moody's Economy.com (economy.com) points to the fact that while the outlook for 2010 appears inviting, there's a catch; unemployment. With a rate of 10%: which is expected to go higher, all the attractive low mortgage rates are of no value if you don't have a stable job. He predicts that home prices will not bottom out until the third quarter of 2010, after losing 37% (peak to trough) based on the S&P/Case-Shiller National Home Price Index (standardandpoors.com); that leaves a 10% decline ahead for 2010. At the top of his list of worries are foreclosures — specifically that

> 66 Most of [the tax credit] is simply shifting sales from one period to another. It doesn't get rid of the fundamental problem; there's still a glut of houses. 99

DR. PATRICK NEWPORT
Economist, IHS Global Insight

the millions of loans that are in foreclosure or headed there can't or won't be modified. That number he estimates to be nearly 2.4 million, which the banks will start putting on the market more aggressively during the first half of the year, resulting in a flood of lower priced houses that will drag prices down.

SUMMARY

The accuracy of everyone's forecasts depends on many things concerning the economy and their views are widely varying, but there is one thing upon which almost all of the experts agree: Though the housing market is most definitely impacted by the national economy, at the end of the day it is local and needs to be analyzed locally. There are charts, graphs, studies and opinions from every corner that reflect the sometimes dramatic differences in varying markets across the country.

Yes, you need to be fully aware of what is influencing the market at the national level but you can't let that overwhelm and confuse you — don't just read the national headlines. They will never replace a good blog that covers the local market in detail. You are the one that needs to understand the critical elements that are impacting your customers — right where they live. It's a great opportunity to step up and provide the solid professional counsel they desperately need and want.

> " The slowdown in many housing markets has created a much longer transaction window with additional opportunities for real estate agents to market to them. "

STEVE BERKOWITZ
CEO, MOVE, Inc.

Here are a few key elements to keep your eyes on:

- **Long-Term Mortgage Rates.** If the Fed begins raising interest rates, it will have an impact in a number of areas in the housing market. Higher rates could affect the large number of ARMs that are due to reset. As we go to press it would appear that they will not go over 6% in 2010 but they bear watching: Keep an eye on long-term Treasury yields. Also watch the action the U.S. Department of Housing and Urban Development (HUD; hud.gov) takes concerning FHA insurance premiums that will impact first-time homebuyers; 80% of FHA-backed loans.

- **The Shadow Inventory.** If banks begin dumping REOs on the market at significantly reduce prices, the impact will be very significant. There are several keys to this issue to watch, including the credit market, unemployment rates and what happens in the commercial real estate market. Keep your eye on the foreclosure market and

what the industry is doing to smooth out the wrinkles in the short sale process in light of the Home Affordable Modification Program (HAMP) guidelines released in November 2009.

- **Federal Subsidy Programs.** No matter whether these programs are extended or closed down, the housing market will feel the impact. The FTHBC and the Fed's security purchase programs have been propping up the market and removing them will have an initial dampening effect. Extending them will most certainly prolong the recovery as the housing market needs to stand on its own two feet if it is ever going to enjoy a genuine recovery. The first quarter of 2010 should tell us a lot.

- **Commercial Real Estate Market.** We reviewed this market in detail in Commercial Real Estate Overview. This is a nightmare that has been building for a long time as the banks and financial institutions have avoided taking a hit in hopes that unemployment will turn around and resolve the problem. That isn't going to happen in the near term and they are going to have to face the problem. There are sure to be some ripple effects that will impact the residential market, a further drying up of credit for one.

- **The Job Market.** Simply put, this is critical for the recovery of the housing market and any significant movement in the level of unemployment in either direction will have an impact on the health of the market. Again, this is a very local issue with a direct impact on you.

- **Consumer Behavior.** One of the key issues concerning the growth of the housing market going forward will be the behavior of consumers. The large losses in wealth they have suffered at the hands of reduced house values, losses in the stock market and unemployment have severely constrained spending. It is a complex issue that will require attention to be paid to multiple elements outside the real estate industry. Keep an eye on how the commercial real estate market fares in the months ahead, specifically retail trends. There are those that see a glimmer of hope in retail, and that's a good sign.

decade ahead.

 TAKE AWAY

As with all predictions, especially economic ones, there are many different and conflicting opinions. The experts, while agreeing on some basic facts are still uncertain about the potential impact of a number of major issues.

One group clearly sees deflation in the coming years as tied to weak residential and commercial real estate values. At the same time another group sees major inflationary pressure resulting from highly aggressive monetary policy and huge deficits.

It's hard to pick sides, especially when so many key actions, decisions and positions taken by the government can so easily impact the direction and the result. Although there are many other pieces to the puzzle, from our perspective, unemployment is at the top of the list. If the government will focus on getting Americans back to work, it will cure a lot of ills.

As real estate professionals we all know that the inherent value of housing will recover and over time will once again become a strong, healthy asset. But the short term increases enjoyed near the end of 2009 aren't the indications that we are looking for.

While we wait for more definitive facts and guidance as to exactly when the housing market will rebound, we need to remember that there will still be a very healthy 5.0 to 5.5 million existing home sales in 2010 and that there isn't any reason that you can't get your share of those sales.

More often than not, fortunes and great companies are born or built during difficult times. Review the Swanepoel Super Seven Trends following these three overviews and see how best you can use this advanced fast-forward into the future to help you prepare for the

Commercial Real Estate

Impact of the Ticking Time Bomb

INTRODUCTION

Over the years this Report has limited its research and comments to the residential real estate sector and for the most part left the commercial sector to others. But with the impact the $6.4 trillion commercial real estate (CRE) market is having on the economy it now also impacts the residential real estate brokerage business.

Historically, CRE has more often than not followed a predictable pattern every five to 10 years:

- Prices rise;
- Developers expand supply;
- Vacancies increase as supply increases;
- Owners default;
- Banks forced to foreclose;
- Vacancies decrease as product is absorbed;
- Market returns.

However, this time has been different as an oversupply of money pushed the CRE over the edge.

The commercial sector has become a ticking time bomb. Net absorption of space is down and falling as vacancy rates across the board are increasing. The fact that banks are tightening their lending requirements, commercial mortgage backed securities (CMBS) — which were responsible for roughly 50% of the CRE financing market — and money from Wall Street are no longer available, is being reflected in the rising number of commercial properties in default, foreclosure or bankruptcy.

> **"** The most prominent area of risk for rising credit losses at FDIC-insured institutions during the next several quarters is in CRE lending. **"**

SHEILA BLAIR
Chairwoman, Federal Deposit Insurance Corporation (FDIC)

POOR PROJECTIONS

When the White House Office of Management and Budget (whitehouse.gov/omb) and the Obama Administration made their assumptions concerning the federal budget and the anticipated unemployment

COMMERCIAL CREDIT FREEZE

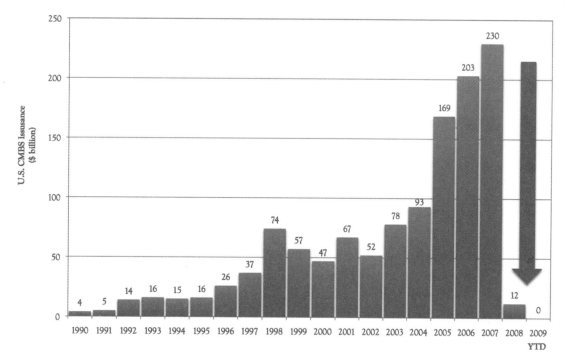

Source: Lawrence Yun, NAR

rate, they missed the mark on both accounts. Unemployment remains high and the federal deficit has ballooned. As of mid-2009 it stood at $992 billion as opposed to $319 billion at the same point in 2008. More troubling is the fact that the deficit has been primarily financed through public borrowing — $7 trillion as of June 2009 (a 21% increase) — all of which is impacting the ability of the CRE market to avoid its slide down the recession's slope.

> **❝** We haven't yet seen the worst of the effects of the recession on the commercial markets; that's still to come. **❞**

STUART SAFT
Partner, Dewey & Leboeuf LLP

Every week the industry watches as CRE takes down another community or regional bank. In October GMAC Commercial Mortgage, a one-time primary commercial real estate lender, filed for bankruptcy. It simply ran out of time and could no longer hold back its imploding commercial debt load. GMAC Commercial is just the beginning. The road ahead for commercial real estate is, to say the least, going to be a long and rough one.

In the '90s, the real estate crisis was the result of over investment and over building, but this time around it's all about cheap credit, which artificially bid up existing commercial properties. Today that has resulted in a problem that, like an ocean wave, is growing in size as it rolls toward the shoreline. At the close of 2009 there was an estimated $400 billion in commercial real estate mortgages coming due with no credit available for refinancing.

It all started with the financial crisis and a severe loss of liquidity, which began driving up capitalization rates (the ratio between the net operating income produced by an asset and its original purchase price or its current market value). The chart reflects the rising Cap Rates demanded by investors for various property types, which in turn inversely reflect the market value for the property. The higher the Cap Rate, the lower the value of the property. As the Cap Rate rises, there is a reflected loss of equity on the part of the owner. When this is added to the lack of available credit, the result is a much lower value. Moody's REAL Commercial Property Price Indices (rcanalytics.com) reports that CRE prices have declined 32.8% from a year ago, 40% from two years ago. For many commercial properties (as in the residential sector) the point of zero or negative equity

CAP RATES

	Cap Rate August 2009 (%)	Expected Cap Rate December 2010 (%)	Expected Cap Rate Shift (Basis Points)
Full-Service Hotels	9.59	10.08	+49
Limited-Service Hotels	9.71	10.15	+45
Power Centers	8.66	9.11	+45
Regional Malls	8.25	8.70	+45
Suburban Office	8.85	9.28	+44
Neighborhood/Community Shopping Centers	8.32	8.72	+39
Apartments: High Income	7.54	7.91	+36
Central City Office	8.03	8.39	+36
R&D Industrial	8.70	9.03	+33
Apartments: Moderate Income	7.64	7.90	+26
Warehouse Industrial	8.30	8.54	+24

Source: PriceWaterhouseCoopers & Urban Land Institute Study

has been reached.

THE UNDERLYING PROBLEM

But now an even more fundamental problem emerges as tenants are vacating spaces due to the deteriorating economy, a loss of income attributed to the number-one issue facing America today: unemployment. Since December 2007 the U.S. has lost nearly 7.2 million jobs. In October 2009 unemployment hit 10.2%, the highest since April 1983. It represented 15.7 million unemployed Americans, up from 15.1 million in September. Since the beginning of the recession the number of unemployed Americans has risen by a factor of 8.2 million.

According to Real Estate Econometrics (reeconometrics.com) the mean duration of unemployment as of the fourth quarter of 2009 was 26.9 weeks, which was up from 26.2 weeks in September. Thus, the average person has been out of work for more than six months. Also of particular interest to the real estate industry is that the unemployment rate for heads of households 24 years old and younger, according to the Wharton School of the University of Pennsylvania, rose from 14.9% to

15.6%. This group is made up almost exclusively of renters and forms the biggest potential pool for first-time homebuyers.

There is also a hidden factor in the unemployment figures provided by the government. When we include unemployed individuals that have looked for work in the last four weeks, discouraged workers that have looked in the past year and part-time workers who want full-time work, that figure jumps to 17.5%.

> " The commercial real estate loan is dead in the water. A severe ongoing credit crunch in commercial lending is hampering the economic recovery. "

DR. LAWRENCE YUN
Chief Economist, NAR

This figure is important because it represents the amount of labor that needs to be absorbed before new jobs can be created. The higher this figure, the longer it will take to stabilize the market and the longer the delay before the economy can once again enjoy true economic growth. According to an October report by Reis, Inc. (reis.com), a leading provider of CRE

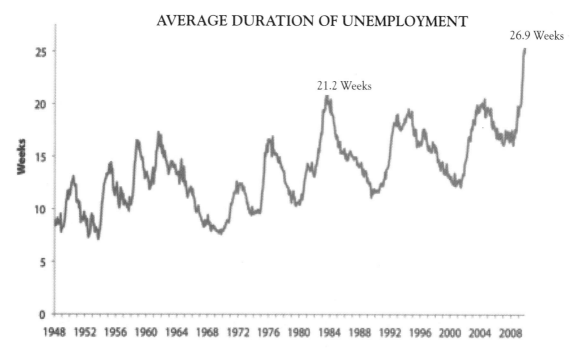

Source: Bureau of Labor Statistics

performance data, this recession is deeper and wider than any recession since the Great Depression and it will take at least 18 to 24 months to recover.

>  The Commercial Real Estate Market won't fully recover until 2020. ""

 KENNETH P. RIGGS JR.
CEO, Real Estate Research

This is especially critical because the commercial sector provides over nine million jobs and funds millions of dollars in the federal, state and local economies in the form of tax revenue. At the local level, this can represent as much as 70¢ of every dollar in the budget and the area being hit the hardest is the retail sector, which provides a key factor in the local budget: sales tax revenue. As the unemployment rate soars, retail sales decline; if the consumers don't have jobs, they don't spend.

THE CURRENT STATE OF AFFAIRS

As would be expected, the rising number of distressed sales have resulted in falling prices and negative equity in the industry. Barclays PLC (barclays.com) reports that there are $270 billion of mortgages on stores, apartment complexes and office buildings alone that need to be refinanced in 2009, all in the face of tightened lending standards and less available credit. Real Capital Analytics (rcanalyatics.com) reported that midway through 2009 commercial properties valued over $108 billion were in default, foreclosure or bankruptcy, double the

Why Dubai Matters
BusinessWeek, December 14, 2009

… "Dubai shows that if you are part of the global economy, you do well; you don't have to have oil." David Aaron, Director [of] Rand Center for Middle East Public Policy.

… [L]ax rules ushered in wild speculation. With real estate prices rising at a double-digit annual clip, investors made a killing buying apartments with low deposits and quickly flipping them.

… [W]hen the credit crunch came, buyers fled and developers saw their cashflow dry up. Hardest hit was Nakheel, a subsidiary of Dubai World that created the iconic Palm Island Real Estate Development off the coast. It has $8 billion in debt and $13 billion in other liabilities, reports Barclays.

… [T]here are many different companies and companies within companies, but the Dubai government owned 100% of Dubai World.

CITYCENTER … Dubai World and MGM Mirage are partners on this $8.5 billion Las Vegas development, which includes 67 acres of hotels and condominiums, as well as a casino and shopping center. The largest ever privately financed construction project in the U.S. may be one of the easiest assets for Dubai World to sell as it has a relatively small debt load.

W UNION SQUARE … Dubai World, which paid a pricey $1 million per guest room for New York's W Union Square, may lose control of the hotel when some of its debt goes to auction this month (December 2009).

… Dubai World faces some steep losses on any sales. The company paid $1 billion for Barneys New York in 2007, and earlier in 2009, bankers valued the retailer at less than half that.

… Abu Dhabi will keep a close watch on the evolving process as the emirate has agreed to provide as much as $15 billion in financial support to Dubai.

level at the same time in 2008. Also as of October 2009, distress sales represented approximately 25% of all transactions, up from 18% in September and 13% in August.

Deutsche Bank (db.com) reported that banks have $1.7 trillion of CRE loans and more than one-fifth of those securitized in 2007 (peak of the boom) could be wiped out. Their report also noted that defaulting loans securitized between 2000 and 2008 could reach $236 to $291 billion, projecting investor losses between $66.2 and $87.5 billion with the largest showing up in 2012 as five year loans made in 2007 begin to show up. It is their belief that 60% of these loans will be un-financeable without substantial equity infusion. They estimate total losses in the coming years could be as high as $90 billion with construction losses near $140 billion. The result — a lot of keys are going to be dropped on the bankers' desks, bankers that may very well not be in a position to pick them up.

amount of debt, there can only be one result: lower prices. Moody's Investors Service (moodys.com) summed it up by reporting that CRE prices have fallen 32.8% from a year ago, 40% from two years ago. Deutsche Bank goes further and estimates that values could lose as much as 50% from their peak in 2007.

Whatever the road ahead has in store one thing is certain: It won't be traveled quickly.

NEXT STEPS

CRE fundamentals continue to deteriorate as the economy struggles to find equilibrium, driving vacancies up and net operating incomes down. The industry also finds itself waiting for the other shoe to drop, as new monetary policies are forcing banks to give up "pretending" and "extending." The industry is overleveraged and the only answer is to pay down the debt.

" A potential wave of defaults in commercial real estate may present a 'difficult' challenge for the economy, without committing to additional steps to aid the market. "

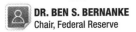
DR. BEN S. BERNANKE
Chair, Federal Reserve

Foresight Analytics (foresightanalytics.com) estimates that approximately 500 banks with assets less than $1 billion are thinly capitalized and have too much exposure to CRE; some 3,000 have CRE loans exceeding 300% of their total risk capital. Supporting those numbers, the Federal Reserve (federalreserve. gov) reported that the 'delinquency rate' for commercial loans, as of the third quarter of 2009, was 8.74%, 8.6 times over its low of 1.01% in the first quarter of 2006. At the same time, the charge-off rate has increased 43 times from .01% to 2.58% over the same time period.

In short, this all adds up to the fact that when you couple a loss of equity with the unavailability of leverage to make purchases, along with a huge

...If it were only that simple.

Faced with $12 trillion of government bailouts and guarantees — government spending now accounts for 26% of the U.S. economy — CRE is in for a long struggle. The government is financing nine out of 10 mortgages as well as most credit cards and auto purchases. Without unwinding all this government involvement the road back for CRE is going to be a long and difficult one.

The reality of change is hard because it usually indicates that something isn't working and needs to be fixed. In real estate, both the commercial and residential sectors are broken and share the same need in order to be fixed: employment. When America once again gets back to work and the residential

---

sector starts increasing housing production and reducing the inventory of unsold properties, CRE will benefit; retail follows rooftops. But in the face of the wave of maturing commercial loans ($6.2 billion in 2011 and 2012) and an environment of tighter lending standards and falling property values, many analysts believe a total recovery could take the better part of a decade. Just the commercial loans made in 2007 will be enough to strain the system as over 80% of them were packaged into bonds and will not qualify for refinancing.

In the meantime, equity continues to sit on the bench as the banks continue to dance around the issue. Deep declines have many borrowers on the verge of being wipe outed, which will force banks to deal with massive writedowns on their balance sheets. But the banks won't be able to play the ostrich much longer; it's only a matter of time before new policies force them to take their heads out of the sand. Reality has a way of accomplishing that.

In the face of some $3 trillion in CRE debt — three times what it was in the 90s — the potential for losses across the board are tremendous. But it's not the debt alone that poses a huge economic hurdle for the industry. The debt issue is the result of problems with the companies that own or lease the buildings, problems caused in no small measure by unemployment.

Through the fourth quarter of 2009 a total of 140 banks had failed, compared to just 25 in all of 2008. Foresight Analytics estimated that as a result of the ongoing downturn in CRE the U.S. banking sector could see as much as $250 billion in losses — enough to cause another 700 banks to fail. Banks have found themselves without any safety margin and, for the most part, have pushed the problem forward by extending loans as they become due, even those in default. Without the lifeblood of debt financing, coupled with deteriorating fundamentals — rising vacancies, falling rents and declining net operating income — CRE is unlikely to begin stabilizing until late 2010 or 2011. Many are pushing for the government to take some action but any action it could take would only delay the outcome. History has proven that government subsidies are always much easier to establish than curtail and there are already too many in place.

But on the other hand, there is opportunity.

NETWORKING AND KNOWLEDGE

If you view your glass as half-full and want to take advantage of the opportunity then you may want to get involved in the commercial sector. A

The Real Estate Drag On GE
BusinessWeek, October 5, 2009

… [I]n 2008 General Electric's commercial real estate business made a $1.1 billion profit. Now, even with signs of the broader economy improving, analysts estimate it could be five years before the unit earns another cent.

… [B]y the end of 2008 the company owned 3,200 properties and held the loans on an additional 4,800, altogether worth some $84 billion as of June — more than all the others with the exception of Wells Fargo and Bank of America according to research firm SNL Financial.

… GE is crashing along with the rest of the industry. Delinquent and bad loans climbed sharply to 2.9% in June from 0.4% in December. The weakness will weigh on the entire company.

… [T]he values on GE's properties continue to slide. It paid $2.2 billion for a set of office and other commercial buildings in Canada at the peak of the market. Among them: a 249,000-square-foot building in midtown Toronto whose vacancy rate is nearly 30%; they are worth about 25% less today.

good place to start may be with the NAR Realtors® Commercial Alliance (RCA), which serves the needs of the commercial market. Organizations within the RCA that support the more than 81,000 NAR members that offer commercial services — over 60,000 are already members of the RCA — include:

- **CCIM Institute** (ccim.com). A Certified Commercial Investment Member (CCIM) is a recognized expert in the disciplines of commercial and investment real estate. More than 9,000 professionals hold the CCIM designation across North America and more than 30 countries. Nearly 9,000 additional professionals are pursuing the CCIM designation.

- **Institute of Real Estate Management** (irem.org). IREM is the only professional real estate management association serving both the multi-family and commercial real estate sectors. Its credentialed membership programs include the Certified Property Manager (CPM), the Accredited Residential Manager (ARM), the Accredited Commercial Manager (ACoM) and the Accredited Management Organization (AMO).

- **Realtors® Land Institute** (rliland.com). The Realtors® Land Institute offers programs and services designed to provide superior land education and professional development programs, encourage open knowledge sharing and interaction among members, develop networking and referral opportunities and serve as a voice in Washington on land-related issues through its affiliation with the NAR.

- **Society of Industrial and Office Realtors®** (sior.com). The Society is the leading professional commercial and industrial real estate association. With more than 3,000 members, SIOR represents today's most knowledgeable, experienced and successful commercial real estate brokerage specialists. Real estate professionals who have earned the SIOR designation are recognized as the most capable and experienced brokerage practitioners in any market. SIOR designees can hold the following specialty designations: industrial, office, sales manager, executive manager or advisory service.

- **Counselors of Real Estate** (cre.org). In the commercial real estate world, only 1,100 real estate advisors are able to call themselves Counselors of Real Estate. It is a designation for a select few who have been recognized by their peers, employers and clients for their commitment, knowledge, experience, wisdom and integrity in the real estate marketplace. No matter the size or scope of an assignment, Counselors leverage their experience to assess the past, present and future and provide sound solutions on the many diversified issues encountered in the broad field of real estate.

✅ TAKE AWAY

Along with the challenges, there will be huge opportunities for both investors and those real estate professionals engaged in the market.

On a large scale, Real Estate Investment Trusts (REITs) are already positioning themselves to take advantage of low market values and pick up properties at bargain-basement prices. In addition, the market anticipates a new wave of Initial Public Offerings (IPOs) by private investors. These are the only two sources of new money on the horizon at this time — money that is desperately needed to fill the credit void.

On a smaller scale, individual investors and small groups of investors are beginning to take a hard look at not only smaller commercial properties but REOs on the residential side. Any time credit is lacking and equity is being lost, those with cash have always done very well and while the regulators are bracing for more bank failures, more opportunities to purchase property at discounted prices emerging every day.

Have we reached the bottom?

The facts would indicate that we have not, that there is still a tough road ahead. But the market is encouraging and those with cash are beginning to stir; it has to start with someone seeing the upside. If improvement in the residential sector can be sustained without governmental subsidies and if unemployment can be turned around, then CRE may just see the graph turn upward in 2010/11. The day of reckoning for CRE is at hand as the parties involved begin to face up to the reality of the losses they have incurred. And that, as it always has, opens the door to opportunity.

Social Media

Continual Confusion, Infinite Innovation

and Endless Opportunities

Note to Reader

This chapter is an overview of the trends that are shaping Social Media. This overview does not in any way discuss the most important platforms, strategies, tactics or action plans required to master Social Media. Those are covered in detail in the 100-page *2010 Swanepoel SOCIAL MEDIA Report*. Details on the *2010 Swanepoel SOCIAL MEDIA Report* are at the end of this Report.

INTRODUCTION

Co-founder of socialmedia.com, Seth Goldstein, says that we are witnessing a profound change in the media and advertising industries due to the emergence of Social Media. Companies that did not exist ten years ago, like Facebook (facebook.com) and Twitter (twitter.com), have captured a significant share of the attention from traditional publishers.

Even at the moment when the media begins to master the basics of Social Media with blogging, the social graph, search engine optimization and cost-per-impression (CPM) yield management, a new set of consumer behaviors — extensive use of mobile devices, location-based services, mixed reality concoctions and Web 3.0 apps — dives into the mix. The game has changed. The new game is called the Golden Triangle and here are its players: Social Content Production, Mobile Media and Real-Time Information.

2009 saw a shifting opinion not only in how information was consumed but also by whom it was controlled. Gone are the days when news corporations and television studios controlled all the information. With the advent of Social Media, information has not only become freely available, it's freely sourced.

SOCIAL CONTENT PRODUCTION

Email of the Moment" and "Direct Marketing for the Decade" are but a few nicknames that have been given to Social Media. It comes as no surprise that the evolution has gone from a quiet social college experience to a completely social everything experience in both marketing and business, where its growth has been staggering.

The *2009 Swanepoel TRENDS Report* mentioned the growing popularity of microblogging and its high profile champion, Twitter. In 2008 Twitter grew rapidly, ending the year with five million Tweeple (Twitter people). The next year it exploded with a large influx of adult users and companies, growing to a total of over 23 million people, according to Compete (compete.com). TwitStat (twitstat.com) estimates that 80% of users do not access Twitter through the website but rather through other clients (including mobile devices), which may account for a lack of growth on the actual Twitter website. However, Twitter broke five billion tweets in October 2009, up from one billion tweets in November 2008, barely a year ago.

> 66 Social Media today is a pure mess: it has become a collection of countless features, tools, and applications fighting for a piece of the pie. 99
>
> **RAVIT LICHTENBERG**
> Founder and Chieft Strategist, Ustrategy.com

YouTube (youtube.com), the largest video sharing site in the world, grew to over one billion views daily by the fourth quarter of 2009 with over 11,500 views per second while Hitwise (hitwise.com) claims that Facebook currently accounts for 6% of all U.S. Internet visits.

Although the growth of social networks continues and the large influx of new content production is something akin to an animal stampede, new content is not solely a result of the adoption of these services and networks by the mainstream, by media

---

or by mobile devices. In a study by Hitwise, visits from individuals 55 and older have increased 77%. Individuals 35 to 54 using Social Media jumped over 60% in 2009, as per Forrester (forrester.com). The adoption rate no longer makes it a kid's game; it is a business opportunity.

> **44** 2009 was the year real estate and marketing realized Social Media is now a part of Internet marketing and the wave of the future. **77**
>
>
> **CHRISTINE MCNAUGHT**
> Broker/REALTOR, Windermere Prestige Properties

According to the Harris Poll (harrispollonline.com), nearly half (48%) of adults have some form of social networking presence in either MySpace or Facebook with 16% of adults updating their page daily. With the growth of social networks there has been some discussion about whether these sites may, at some point, become a threat to search engines such as Yahoo! (yahoo.com) or Google (google.com). Looking ahead, utilization of social networks is expected to continue to dramatically increase in 2010. It is however, the methods of usage and consumption that will change.

MOBILE MEDIA

With the complete outbreak of modern smartphones with location-based services, Wi-Fi capabilities and online access that has made Social Media become more accessible with each passing day. According to a study by eMarketer (emarketer.com), mobile Internet users are estimated to increase over 30% year-over-year from 2009 to 2010 to include over 657.2 million users worldwide. Mobile social networking will grow to include approximately 225 million users by the end of 2010, up from 141 million in 2009 — a 60% increase year-over-year. That means that social networking is one of the fastest-growing activities among mobile users and has become a significant driver of Internet usage on mobile devices.

The *2008 Swanepoel TRENDS Report* outlined the evolution of online communities and social networks. At that time, nearly a quarter of the world's population — about 1.4 billion people — used the Internet on a regular basis according to a study done by International Data Corporation (IDC; idc.com). That number is expected to increase by 36% before 2012 to 1.9 billion users, with an annual increase of 125 million users. Unlike Internet growth, the IDC found that in 2008 roughly 40% of all Internet users worldwide — approximately 546 million (8% of the world's population) — had mobile Internet access. That figure was nearly twice as many as there were in 2006.

Furthermore, the forecast shows that the number of mobile Internet users worldwide in 2012 will surpass 1.5 billion, and according to Juniper Research (juniperresearch.com) the number of mobile Internet users will exceed 1.7 billion in 2013. This would correlate to over 20% of the world's population having access to the Internet via a mobile device by 2012. It is easy to see why the mobile device will soon be the primary connection tool to the Internet.

LOCATION-BASED SERVICES (LBS)

With the popularity of modern smartphones on the rise, Pete Cashmore, Founder and CEO of Mashable (mashable.com), notes that 2010 will find location-based services (LBS) becoming the breakout services of the year as these devices are fueled by the ubiquity of GPS technology.

JLSConnect

Seattle-based John L Scott Real Estate, in association with Microsoft, built their own social network: JLSConnect.

Powered by Microsoft Silverlight, it integrates various 'cloud computing' services including LiveID, Live Contacts, Live Presence, Live Messenger and Virtual Earth on JohnLScott.com

These services are commonly delivered to mobile devices but with some adaption can also be accessed from laptops, various handhelds or any Internet-capable device. Wikipedia lists some LBSs as:

- Requesting the nearest business or service such as an ATM or restaurant;

- Accessing turn-by-turn navigation to any address;

- Locating people on a map displayed on a mobile phone;

> **❝ What might appear as an important communication from real estate professionals may in fact be a nuisance to an increasingly educated consumer. ❞**

SCOTT LEFORCE
President, Realty World Northern CA & NV

- Receiving alerts, such as notification of a sale on gas or traffic warnings;

- Location-based mobile advertising.

An increasing number of mobile applications are taking advantage of the built-in LBS capability that is increasingly a standard feature in mobile devices. ABI Research (abiresearch.com) expects LBS application downloads to increase to more than 260 million in 2010 and to reach almost two billion by 2014. The main drivers of the LBS revolution are the sudden rise in popularity of a new generation of touch-screen GPS-enabled smartphones, combined with a wide range of application stores launched by handset and mobile operating system vendors, says ABI Research practice director Dominique Bonte.

Accessing information about nearby buildings, restaurants, landmarks or other features is now commonplace. Location-based services are

increasingly using social context to locate people nearby — people known or unknown to the user — who share interests or experiences in common. This allows for social networking and social reviews to tie into location-based inquiries. As LBSs continue to develop in 2010, specialized applications will see a focus on education through the delivery of relevant location-based information and the geo-tagging (adding GPS coordinates to content) of captured data.

Common applications for location-based services in use today include advertising, news, social networking and similar services. Following this trend the popularity of social networking continues to create increasing demand for access anywhere, anytime.

THE RISE OF REAL-TIME

As Social Media and mobile technology grow and become intertwined, so will the need for more information delivered at an even faster rate. In fact, many Social Media sites like Twitter and Facebook already provide a real-time or near real-time flow of information: Commentary in YouTube is much the same. Moreover, the improvements in information processing are not simply limited to social networks or web searches. Tie in location-based services— mobile media's trump card — and social networking is bound for a whole new dimension. Marta Kagen, the U.S.

> **❝ Many people use [Twitter] for professional purposes — keeping connected with industry contacts and following news... [B]ecause it's a one-to-many network and most of the content is public, it works for this better than a social network that's optimized for friend communication. ❞**

EVAN WILLIAMS
Twitter Co-Founder & Chief Executive

managing director for Espresso-Brand Infiltration (brandinfiltration.com), says that real-time reviews will scare many brands and that it will foster in a new beta, or always changing mindset in web and mobile development. In short, it is the introduction of a visible perpetual beta to signify the continuous improvement and innovation on a global scale.

Imagine searching for a local venue and having the search results provide a set of "live dispatches" by theme, brand or any other category where, as Ginny Cooper of the Cooper Group (mycoopergroup.com) notes, ready-to-buy consumers are able to tap into a live stream of (first-hand) experiences from fellow consumers. With real-time content in search results, search engines will also become social with information from social network friends and other web surfers. Those dismissing the value of the underlying concept — real-time information — appear to be increasingly in the minority according to InformationWeek (informationweek.com).

Companies will quickly master the art of real-time. For example, Google in December 2009, introduced real-time information in its search results through a series of partnerships — including Twitter, Facebook, MySpace, FriendFeed, Jaiku and Identi.ca.

With its new Twitter relationship, Google now shows a user's tweets alongside internal search results. This update follows Google's practice of providing related web results next to corporate search results and also displays Google's prowess at keeping social networks at bay.

However, the value of real-time information is not in the buzz or the improvements in web searching. The value to produce results moments after content has been published, or even the inclusion of social networking in search results is but only the beginning. With growth of social networks and social features such as opinions, sharing and reviews integrated into

almost anything online, the increasing capabilities of the online user experience suggest a unique development for Social Media as it envelopes itself permanently into the Web in 2010 — Augmented or Mixed Reality.

THE REAL WORLD GAINS POPULARITY

Dan Zarella, a Social Media & Viral Maketing Scientist for Hubspot (hubspot.com), says that with Augmented Reality and mobile Social Media the real world will be important again. Augmented Reality, as defined by Wikipedia (wikipedia.org), is a term for a live, direct or indirect view of a physical real-world environment whose elements are merged with (or augmented by) virtual computer-generated imagery creating a Mixed Reality. More commonly it is the application and complete power of the Web, including all Social Media, searching, reviews, etc., integrated into daily life beyond the laptop or office computer. It is the overlay of graphics onto a video stream or a heads-up display. It is a new way to see the real world.

As this 'Mixed Reality' intertwines with mobile applications that seek to improve real-time information searches, much like real-time turn-by-turn GPS directions, the social sphere will find a new home in mobility, with social reviews and ratings as more individuals seek answers on the go. This new Mixed Reality is but a step in the next wave of Internet browsing, information search and general queries. No need to find a computer for a Google search regarding the quality of nearby restaurants or details about the house down the street; consumers will begin to use camera phones to display restaurant ratings, reviews and menus from location-and-image-

#1 in the World

Who would have predicted that China would end the first decade of the 21st Century as the world's largest Internet user. It started the year 2000 with an estimated eight million users and today, at the end of 2009, has surpassed 360 million users, more than the total U.S. population. And although the Chinese government has prevented various popular Social Media networks such as Facebook and Twitter, the Chinese still use the Internet for all the regular things we do such as talking, networking, shopping and sharing.

based services. Possibilities will even extend into MLS (Multiple Listing Service) searches as consumers seek to gain information on the go. Projected by an ABI Research study, handheld platforms will transform the Augmented Reality ecosystem with associated revenue increasing from $6 million in 2008 to over $350 million in 2014.

THE GOLDEN TRIANGLE

As the concept of the Golden Triangle — Social Content Production, Mobile Media and Real-Time Information — begins to weave together and as consumers move away from the typical Social Media platforms and opt for a 'more valuable' real-world experience, innovation in Augmented Reality will show us that 2009 was the year to learn about Social Media and that 2010 will be the year to optimize it.

Social Media is already part of mainstream media, but it is even moving beyond the mainstream and becoming a marketing tool and utility. It is a key part of your business.

SOCIAL BEYOND MAINSTREAM

A study by The Economist (economist. com), showed that traditional advertising in 2009 was in a decline with newspapers and magazines leading the way. However, on the positive side digital marketing is increasing with mobile advertising up 18.1% and Internet marketing up 9.2%. A shift is occurring as consumers look for information in new locations. The 2009 Swanepoel TRENDS Report mentioned this shifting opinion and how it has subsequently introduced the power of a single individual. However, we are still plagued with too much information and even in the realm of email 90% of the 200 billion emails sent each day are spam and the convergence of Social Media with Mobile Media will exacerbate the problem of information overload as more content sharing enters the picture.

Take, for example, the New York Times (NYT; nytimes.com), where there are currently three ways to read articles. The first is the newspaper and magazine, which are noticeably in a decline. The second is its website, with online articles, often the primary choice, as seen by the large influx of unique readers (30 million) to online newspapers in the last five years according to the Economist. The third form, and the newest of the three, is the New York Times iPhone application. Although still young and new to the game, there is an increasing trend

> **"** Social Media is a different way of communicating with the traditional sources of business. Just as we moved from the phone to mail to email to Internet and now to Social Media, if you aren't providing a service, it's just another tool that if used improperly yields nothing. **"**
>
> **EARL LEE**
> President, Prudential Real Estate and Relocations

in sharing to move beyond standard circulation, beyond email and going mobile and social. Even YouTube has introduced YouTube Direct, a tool that allows organizations to view, request and rebroadcast YouTube clips.

While the migration continues and more companies are found blogging and tweeting like the NYT or CNN, there are a few things to note as Social Media moves beyond mainstream acceptance and into everyday life:

- **Policies Gain Traction**. Using Social Media as a business tool and marketing platform will eventually lead to a company adopting an online policy program. Social Media Governance (socialmediagovernance.com) currently lists over 100 policies.

- **Integration of Services**. With services such as DataPortability (dataportability.com) and OpenID (openid.net) beginning to work their way through the Web and Social Media, a centralized, unified log-in service that allows for the simplification in Social Media management can't be far off.

- **Social-less Media and Social Business.** Originally designed as a way to communicate on a social level to maintain friendships and relationships, companies are now scaling their operations in true business fashion by leveraging the power of Social Media. Companies such as Best Buy's Twelp Force (twitter.com/twelpforces) use hundreds of employees on Twitter as a customer service platform to effect cost savings through social technology.

SOCIAL MEDIA IN BUSINESS

Businesses are using Social Media like Facebook, LinkedIn and blogging tools like Twitter to form new and lucrative connections with consumers. However, diving in without doing research shows that there are pitfalls when they get it wrong. A Forrester study revealed that online display advertising, which in 2009 stood at $7.83 billion, is expected to rise by 17% annually, ending up around $16.9 billion in 2014. Online search marketing such as that seen on Google or Yahoo!, which currently consume $15.39 billion in spending, will jump by 15%, to $31.59 billion. The increasing shift from traditional media to online is obvious, but a badly thought-out start into the interactive space could do more harm than good.

Most businesses that understand Social Media see it as another arm to their marketing mix and not a sales generator. According to eMarketer, the amount of online ad spending per Internet user is also growing and did, in 2009 for the first time surpass $100 per user. By 2011 advertisers are expected to spend nearly double that amount online per user.

Each Social Media platform has its own necessary level of understanding and each platform has its own characteristics. True success in Social Media means being brave enough to give away your brand, not

> **❝ Today the best agents work with the consumer and the Internet. ❞**
>
> **HELEN HANNA CASEY**
> President, Howard Hanna Real Estate Services

pretending to give it away and keeping control. The balance in content is the million-dollar question. Too much advertising and product pushing is as much of a turnoff as being overly personal — something people do not necessarily want to hear from a business.

Swanepoel SOCIAL MEDIA Report 2010

The *Swanepoel SOCIAL MEDIA Report 2010* is published with the focus of guiding you through the entire Social Media process, from where it came from to where you should start. The Report also covers what you need to do, what tools you should use and what Social Media networks you should join. Other important information includes how to conduct yourself, measure your time, monitor conversations and how to tie it all together into one effective stragegy while still maintaining balance.

As a bonus we have included a step-by-step 10-day Action Plan.

To get your copy of the Report visit RETrends.com and use the promo code — friends — for a significant discount.

TAKE AWAY

The social web is not a fad and as such neither is Social Media. The freedom that the social web introduces is a fundamental shift in how we communicate, interact, collaborate, create, inform ourselves, inform others, prioritize, organize, buy, sell and play. The social web is you. It's your customers, your friends, your family, your employees, your shareholders, your colleagues and everyone else. Social Media represents a new avenue to listen and communicate.

Conversations are taking place about everything including your company, product and service. The discussions are happening right now and as technology improves, the Golden Triangle will become more effective and information will become more readily available.

Yes, it's all happening faster and faster but in the process the value and purpose of using these services are often ignored. Growth in Social Media was phenomenal in 2009 and will only accelerate as the next wave of Social Media interaction moves firmly onto mobile platforms. For more details on using Social Media, please review the *Swanepoel SOCIAL MEDIA Report 2010*.

Some label this growth, innovation or next step in the evolution of the Web as the Golden Triangle or Web 3.0, but in all reality, the next step is: convergence, the convergence of the three key avenues of the Internet – Social Content, Mobile Media and Real-Time Information.

If you don't master Social Media, your competition will.

Book III

Super 7 Trends: Residential Real Estate

Introduction

Definition of a Trend

A generic term used to describe any consistent pattern or change in the general direction of a stock, a market or an industry that over the course of time causes a statistically noticeable change.

Fad or Trend

It is sometimes hard to distinguish between a "Fad" and a "Trend, " between those events that will have longevity and substance compared to those that will fizzle out and fade away. Identifying a trend is not an exact science but rather an art based on facts, patterns, change and time.

What Constitutes a Trend?

Trends are generally not products and services; nor are they the companies that deliver them. They are instead the concepts, beliefs or philosophies — the fundamental reasons that often cause a market to change direction.

Trends are more often than not interwoven with one another and one trend often encapsulates part of another. Trends are frequently born as a result of other events that have changed or shifted a paradigm, allowing the evolution of a new trend.

Trends in Real Estate

Some trends in the real estate industry evolve internally to meet a specific need, while others develop when new products or solutions are created to solve problems that may or may not exist. Many times a successful trend in another industry spills over into the real estate industry and after trial and error it is adopted.

Many new trends do not make it to the Top 7 Trends list. The following factors are taken into consideration when evaluating trends:

- Origin of the concept or trend;
- The driving force behind it;
- Its lifecycle and maturity;
- The industry demand or need for the result;
- Its growth pattern;
- Its potential impact on the industry.

Straddling the Fence

Are You Committed?

OVERVIEW

A recent study for CareerBuilder.com (careerbuilder.com) reported that one in ten Americans surveyed is currently working more than one job and an astounding 61% are living from paycheck to paycheck. The ranks of the real estate industry are no exception.

The slumping economy and housing markets, fueled by fierce competition, are forcing many agents to rethink their career choices. The once heady market now has them scrambling for supplemental income or leaving the industry altogether. History has shown that even in good times, only one in four agents make it past their first year and with the boom days of 2001 to 2006 long gone, the ranks are shrinking by the month.

According to the Association of Real Estate License Law Officials (ARELLO; arello.com) the total number of real estate licensees (active and inactive) in the U.S. in December 2009 was 3,032,244. At the same time, the NAR reported its membership at 1.13 million, a decline from 1.37 million in 2006. Decreasing along with that number has been Realtor® median income; from a high of $49,300 in 2004 to $36,700 in 2008. But while the number of licensees has been declining the share of a fewer number of commissions has also declined. Thus there are many looking for a secondary source of income.

The *NAR 2009 Member Profile* reveals that 76% of all Realtors® indicated that real estate was their only occupation; 26% did not. As would be anticipated, as years of experience increase the percentage also

increases. Another key indicator was the fact that less than half of all Realtors® reported that real estate was their primary source of household income; 44%. Once again those with fewer years in the business are more dependent upon income from outside the real estate industry.

Historically when the market slows real estate agents often turned to the support services such as appraisal, title or insurance to find some additional work. But now, those industries are suffering along with real estate sales and many real estate agents and Realtors® are being forced to look elsewhere to keep the bills paid. It's a fact that is having a significant impact on the industry and poses a serious question — should Realtors® that are working part-time disclose that fact to their clients?

REAL ESTATE IS THEIR ONLY PROFESSION

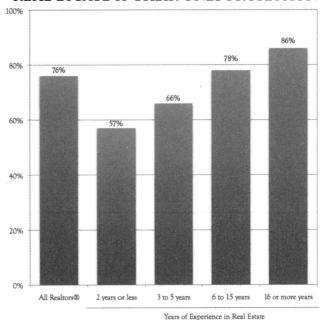

Years of Experience in Real Estate

Source: NAR

REAL ESTATE IS PRIMARY SOURCE OF INCOME FOR HOUSEHOLD

		Liscensed As		Real Estate Experience			
	All Realtors®	Broker/ Broker Associates	Sales Agents	2 years or less	3 to 5 years	6 to 15 years	16 years or more
All Realtors®	44%	53%	37%	22%	32%	48%	57%
Work less than 40 hours per week	22	29	18	10	13	25	33
Work 40 hours or more per week	61	66	56	40	50	64	71

Source: NAR

IMPACT ON CONSUMERS

When real estate agents take on second and third jobs and decide not to disclose that fact to their client it raises questions concerning their level of commitment and service such as:

- What are my Realtor's® priorities?
- Who will handle urgent issues that arise?
- Will I get all the marketing services promised?
- Are my Realtor's® education and skills up-to-date?
- What happens when timing is critical?
- Will my Realtor® completely go out of business?

When a real estate agent is only available during certain hours and the client is anticipating 24/7 service there is a disconnect that can lead to a number of problems, not the least of which is effective and timely communication.

Many real estate agents have successfully held down second jobs for years and have developed systems to ensure that customer needs are met and questions are answered responsibly and effectively. This is usually the result when their primary job and focus is real estate, but the extent to which this changes when real estate is no longer their primary function is the issue facing the industry. No matter whether they think they are successful or unsuccessful in servicing the consumer while juggling dual careers, the impact on the industry is significant. A recent survey revealed that 36% of Realtor® Associations saw an increase in ethics complaints and a 39% increase in arbitration.

IMPACT ON ASSOCIATIONS

Some Realtor® Associations have been asking themselves key questions about the continuing decline in membership and what they can do to turn the tide:

- What should we do about the loss of revenues due to members' inability to renew their memberships and purchase ancillary services/products?
- Should we adjust office hours or the delivery of services online?
- Should there be a new product/service mix to meet the needs of part-time practitioners?
- How do we deal with business practices issues with unavailable agents and brokers?

> ❝ Love it or hate it 2009 was an opportunity to take those steps necessary to running your business effectively again. It took a misguided Wall Street to put Main Street back into a reality based business model. Too bad it will take regulation to put Wall Street in reality with America. ❞

JAMES W. WRIGHT
President, Century 21 All Islands, Hawaii

One of the associations seriously studying this phenomenon is the Chicago Association of Realtors® (CAR; chicagorealtor.com). In association with RealSure, Inc. (realsure.com), the publishers of this Report, during the last half of 2009, CAR conducted a survey of their 56 local associations and, according to Ginger Downs, CAR CEO, the results confirmed that the "dual-career agent" is having an impact on their local associations. While not a national response, the results of this survey of local associations is considered to be very representative of the experiences of associations all across the country. The following summarizes some of the responses from Chicago's local associations regarding their Realtor® members and the actions taken in response:

- 69% of local associations reported that they have Realtors® with second jobs and 84% said this was an increase over 2008.
- Only 27% of Realtors® surveyed by local associations listed real estate as their primary source of income.
- When asked if they have seen an increase in the number of complaints 55% of the local associations noted a general lack of professionalism, 36% saw an increase in ethics complaints and 39% saw an increase in arbitration.

The survey also revealed some very interesting trends concerning dual-career Realtors®:

- Those with good technology usage are responsive, but generally they are not responsive in a timely manner.
- They are asking the other agent in the transaction to assume more responsibility and transactions are taking longer.
- They are asking their Designated Realtor® (DR) or office manager to handle more administrative or promotional activities.

To determine what local associations were doing in light of the growing number of dual-career agents the survey asked what changes, if any, they had made. The table highlights the results.

> **❝** The housing market's long decline has left once-thriving real estate professionals scrambling for supplemental income or changing professions. **❞**

THE WALL STREET JOURNAL

ASSOCIATION CHANGES DUE TO DUAL CAREER AGENTS

Realtor® Association Questions	Yes	No
Have you extended days of service?	21.4%	78.6%
Have you modified services?	82.1%	17.9%
Have you reduced/waived dues/MLS fees or others?	19.6%	80.4%
Have you created payment plan for MLS fees?	39.3%	60.7%
Have you provided some products/services for free?	46.4%	53.6%
Have you provided education during the evening?	46.4%	53.6%
Have you provided more online/self-study courses?	37.5%	62.5%
Have you increased more communication in online/email blasts?	64.3%	35.7%
Have you produced more webcasts/podcasts?	21.4%	78.6%
Have you increased your social networking?	62.5%	37.5%
Have you acquired more technology apps to improve agent field efficiency?	32.1%	67.9%
Have you provided online editable PDF forms?	30.4%	69.6%
Have you provided a showing assistance program?	16.1%	83.9%

Source: CAR

Of particular note was the high percentage of associations that began providing some products/services for free, offering more education in the evening and emphasizing more social networking in an effort to assist these members.

The survey also queried Designated Realtors® (DR) to determine the impact of dual-career agents on them.

IMPACT ON DESIGNATED REALTORS® (DR)

Designated Realtors® disclosed some interesting trends regarding both brokerage companies and brokers individually. In their responses the DRs indicated that 63% of their agents hold a second job; 51% felt that there wasn't a problem; while the other 49% had concerns regarding:

1. Difficulty in communicating effectively;
2. Loss of income due to lower productivity;
3. The need to provide more technology training;
4. Increase in formal complaints filed with association MLS;
5. DR taking over more transaction management;
6. DR providing more support in the areas of technology and promotion;
7. Larger office splits than in the past.

When asked if the DRs themselves held a second job, 51% responded yes, up 21% from a year ago. But more revealing was the fact that a huge number (42%) indicated that they worked more than half the time (20 hours/week) at their second job.

IMPACT ON DUAL CAREER REALTORS®

The decision to leave the real estate industry is a difficult one for most agents but it's not just because they have experienced the benefits of a hot market. The costs of becoming a licensee and a Realtor® are significant, not to mention the annual costs involved — NAR dues, MLS fees, education, operating expenses, etc. As a result, many are very reluctant to simply turn their back on the industry

> " Just as the Unmanned Aerial Vehicles (UAVs) have changed how we fight a war from a remote location, the "real estate internet cloud" has given the consumer the ability to gather the same or better real estate information from their laptop with out using the real estate agent. The real estate model has moved from agent centered to consumer centered. "

JIM NEAR
Operating Principal, Keller Williams Realty Charleston

and walk away. But with an annual net income of $30,900 ($36,700 gross less $5,800 expenses) the average Realtor® is not far above the poverty line, which is $22,000 for a family of four. In fact, according to the *NAR's 2009 Member Profile*, 39% of all Realtors® reported earning less than $25,000, while only 16% reported earning $100,000 or more.

At the same time those who refuse to leave the industry and elect to take on second and third jobs just to stay alive are a huge roadblock in the path of progress. While there are those Realtors® who have developed processes and systems to help them service the consumer, they are by far the minority. For most Realtors®, the pressures and demands of balancing two or more jobs — especially in the current economic climate — are burdens to an industry that's trying to achieve the level of

professional customer service it believes is critical for its survival. A significant part of that burden falls directly on the full-time professionals and the supporting administrative and managerial staff that have to pick up the slack. It's not a recipe the industry can continue to use.

BARRIERS TO ENTRY

The real estate industry is no longer a place for the weak-hearted. The pie is shrinking and it will become increasingly more difficult for the part-time Realtor® or agent to survive. But it's not just about a shrinking market; it's all about what it will take to be successful in that market. In the past it was just a "path to the money," but today it has become a career that requires a new commitment to absorb all of the issues surrounding an evolving and changing marketplace and consumer. There is little time for the distractions associated with maintaining more than one job.

What the industry needs to do first and foremost is drastically restructure its entry-level requirements, as well as those for maintaining a license. It is far too easy to maintain a dual career and that is clearly detrimental to the industry's desire to raise the bar

> " The gap between the producing and non-producing agents and companies is growing at a more rapid pace than ever. The consumers and agents will gravitate to those they perceive to provide the most trusted advice. "

CHRIS READ
Founder, CR Strategies LLC

of professionalism. What the industry needs, if it is going to survive, are serious, well-qualified, full-time professionals who are totally dedicated to servicing the consumer. So does that mean the end of the dual-career agent?

Not in the near future. It is still too easy to maintain a real estate license, which allows many to pursue a secondary source of income. As a result, far too many stay in the real estate business at a relatively low income level, and that isn't going to change until

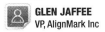

> Consider the estimation that 58% of Realtors® will be retiring in the next 5 -10 years.

GLEN JAFFEE
VP, AlignMark Inc

the licensing and continuing education requirements become tougher. In the meantime the needs of those with dual careers are having an increased impact on the local and state associations as they struggle to keep pace with the changing market and adequately serve an ever increasingly more informed and demanding consumer. As a result, there is more "revenue" pressure being put on associations to assist these Realtors® in order to keep them productive and in the game. As was noted in the survey, 20% of the DRs indicated that 50% of their agents had two jobs and, more importantly, 53% of them want to return to real estate as their number one job. They aren't going to leave the industry easily.

 TAKE AWAY

As those in the industry struggle with defining their role in the future, Realtors® that have chosen to maintain dual-careers face an uphill battle to remain in the game at an effective level. At the same time Realtor® Associations face the challenge of meeting the needs of this growing segment of the industry or face the prospect of further reduced membership numbers and the associated loss of revenue.

Considerations for Associations:

1. Offer more evening and weekend education opportunities as well as more online and/or self-study options, especially in the area of technology training to improve efficiency;

2. Make available more information on services, activities, etc., on the association website and push more information through weekly email blasts;

3. Utilize webinars, webcasts and social networking sites to promote important services, activities and announcements;

4. Develop a mobile application to better connect members to the association website and come out to member offices more frequently to talk about products and services;

5. Post information on job fairs or career days and offer information and/or education on managing dual careers;

6. Offer information and/or education on working with dual career agents.

> Broker profitability has always been and will always be connected inextricably to the consumer of real estate services.

GEORGE C. STEPHENS
Founder & Designated Manager, RealtySnap

Considerations for Realtors®:

1. Answer the soul-searching question: "Do I want a career in real estate?"

2. Make the commitment to do whatever it takes to alleviate the need for a second job;

3. Develop a definitive game plan to acquire the education, skills and technology necessary to be competitive in the market;

4. Establish a solid plan to ensure that your clients' needs are met efficiently, timely and effectively using technology, Realtor® backup, administrative support, etc.;

5. Reveal all facts to your client upfront.

The challenge facing the NAR, state and local Realtor® Associations and brokers alike is not to become co-dependent but to develop the necessary support systems to help that 53% rejoin the industry in full... or get out.

In Search of Innovation

How Do "You" Change the Game?

OVERVIEW

Change is tough. We all know that. It is, however, even harder when decisions that impact change, and thus your future, are made by a group or committee. Some say it is actually impossible and that change invariably comes from external sources. Existing players can invest in game changers, but they can't really be game changers themselves — or so they say.

It is that very premise, which has been proven correct more often than not, that has now been challenged by no one other than a 100-year old, unwieldy association — the National Association of Realtors®.

In August 2009, the NAR instituted the Game Changers Challenge, challenging its 1,400+ local Realtor® Boards, State Association of Realtors® and Institutes, Societies and Councils. They were charged with creating new benefits and the NAR encouraged state and local associations to develop new perspectives towards day-to-day work and to focus on the value of finding new ideas and formulating them to answer the challenge. These game changing ideas must have an impact on the association, a new product, program, process or service that would improve the organization.

Submissions included programs on commercial and international services, education and training, community, events, leadership development, marketing, customer service, technology, networking and social media. More specifically they included: programs focused on neighborhoods, sharing of association resources; lending a hand to our returning war heroes; self-paced education that allows Realtors® to design their own programming; forward thinking technology services; programs and products; enhancing the Realtor® brand; assisting today's homeowner; real time communication; environmental enhancements and training. The goal is to guarantee that the Realtor® of today and tomorrow is on the cutting edge of the industry.

The NAR received over 200 submissions and at its convention in San Diego announced 14 winners who received over $1.7 million to undertake their chosen projects. Each winner was assigned a coach to assist in the development of their project. There were also 22 runners-up who received a total of over $170,000. The remaining submissions received a $500 credit in 2010 to attend a professional development event. In total, the NAR will provide close to $2,000,000 in funding for the Game Changer Program (realtor.org/gamechangers).

The fact that the NAR is doing this during the most challenging economic times we have experienced in decades sends a strong message. The NAR leadership feels that spending money on its members and state and local associations today is priority number one. They view the return on the investment in terms of all these programs in some way changing the way associations, Realtors® and consumers do business.

According to the NAR, the current winners, runners-up and the bright ideas generated have created an idea bank of programs that can be implemented now and for years to come. They represent a broad range of concepts from a diverse group of business leaders that demonstrate new and imaginative ways of responding to the challenges in Realtor® association

> **44** Traditional players often cannot change, but they can invest in the game changers. **77**
>
> **KEN AULETTA**
> Author, Googled: The End of the World As We Know It

management. It is both a short and long-term approach to developing new and enhancing existing programs to make the overall Realtor® experience a better one.

THE WINNING INITIATIVES

Here is an encapsulation of the 14 winning initiatives in alphabetical order:

NAR *Game Changers* CONCEPTS

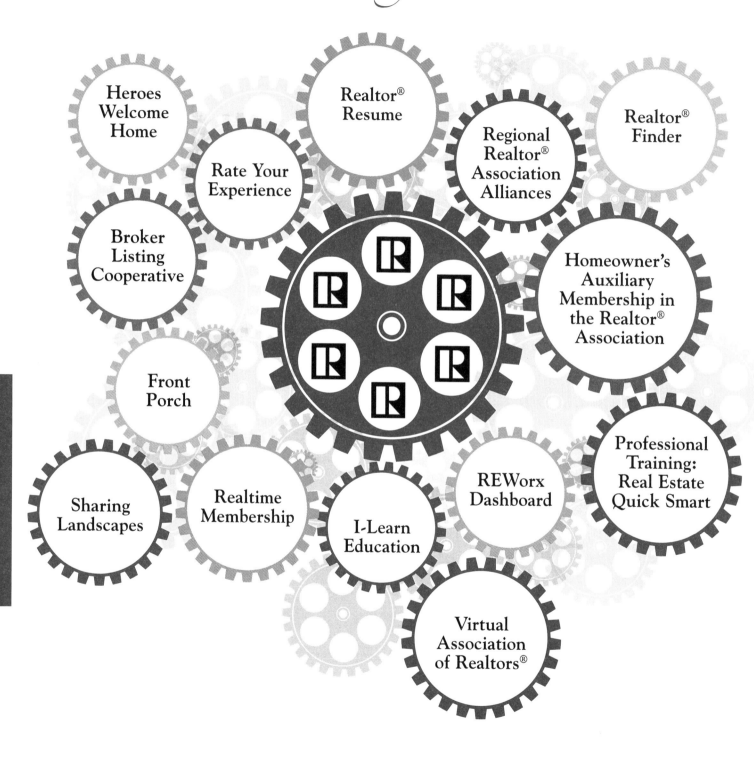

1. Broker Listing Cooperative

Proposed and to be developed by the Metropolitan Indianapolis Board of Realtors®; they will be assisted by Steve Murray of REAL Trends.

This program proposes that the NAR acquires the trademarked term Broker Listing Cooperative® and BLC® for national use. BLC® would:

1. Recapture the culture of a cooperative for its brokers and agents;
2. Set apart the uniqueness of the listing cooperative to consumers.

This would re-brand the listing service.

2. Front Porch

Proposed and to be developed by the Bay East Association of Realtors® in California and Missoula Association of Realtors® in Montana; they will be assisted by Jeremy Conaway of RECON Intelligence Services.

The Front Porch initiative will aim to establish Realtors® as local neighborhood experts and community builders through the development of a website that is community-centered and neighborhood focused. It aims to include blogs, photos, videos and other social media to highlight the experience of living in specific neighborhoods and the collective experience of living in the larger community (e.g., a video showing the walking route to the nearest coffee house).

3. Heroes Welcome Home

Proposed and to be developed by the Chicago Association of Realtors®; they will be assisted by Judith Lindenau of JWL Associates.

Heroes Welcome Home will be an informational program designed to educate Realtors® about the severity of the conditions that returning members of the military experience. Realtors® will learn the needs of these soldiers for specialized housing and will understand how to work with these heroes to identify and locate housing within the city of Chicago. The association will act as the sole contact for the MilitaryHOMEFRONT and Department of Defense without the Department having to inform thousands of Realtors® individually.

4. Homeowner's Auxiliary Membership in the Realtor® Association

Proposed and to be developed by the Sacramento Association of Realtors®; they will be assisted by former NAR Senior Vice President, Nancy Wilson Smith.

This program for sellers and buyers would allow temporary membership in the local association and access to its website. Upon taking a listing, the seller's Realtor® will give membership to the seller. Upon close of a transaction the buyer's Realtor® will give membership to the new home owner. Membership would include access to a website with members-only information on preparing the house for sale, real estate statistics and demographics and new legislation affecting private property rights. Access to affinity programs and discounts at local home improvement stores would be included as well.

5. I-Learn Education

Proposed and to be developed by the Institute of Real Estate Management (IREM); they will be assisted by John Featherston of RISMedia.

I-Learn will be an education program that uses a blended learning environment for members to fulfill their credential requirements. This program will consist of mobile learning such as smartphone modules, podcasts, Social Media, blogs, virtual study groups, self-paced e-learning courses, facilitated online learning, webinars and learning labs as well as live facilitated classrooms. The program will allow members to design their own education programs according to their schedules, learning styles and technology preferences.

6. Professional Training: Real Estate Quick Smart

Proposed and to be tested by the Pinellas Realtors® Organization, Clearwater, Florida; they will be assisted by John Tuccillo of JTA.

For today's challenging business environment Real Estate Quick Smart would be an education program designed to bring newer agents up to speed quickly. While many brokers' resources for training have diminished this program will allow them to offer a "quick smart" program developed by the association that will teach the core elements of the real estate process. New and less experienced agents will gain knowledge and procedural skills based on the proven experience of seasoned professionals. The program will be offered to brokers as a privately labeled, internal education program but would be hosted and managed by the association. This aids the broker and also enhances the association's role as a premier provider of education for real estate professionals.

7. Rate Your Experience

Proposed and to be developed by the Peoria Area Association of Realtors®; they will be assisted by Greg Larson of Clareity Consulting.

Rating is the new advertising. Rate Your Experience would provide a local association a rating site that encompasses all service providers in a real estate transaction including brokerages, real estate licensees, lenders and inspectors. This system could also include a more contemporary method of handling professional standards and dispute resolution, providing a total transaction experience evaluation. Members would be able to use insights from the rating system to improve their own performance and promote their quality services.

8. Realtime Membership

Proposed and to be developed by the Northwest Mississippi Association of Realtors®; they will be assisted by Jeremy Conaway of RECON Intelligence Services.

Realtime Membership Communications will be a multi-choice messaging dashboard created to allow a single message to be instantly delivered

> **❝** The bottom line is that the Game Changers Challenge allowed and required the local boards and associations to think differently. It is an incredibly forward thinking approach to taking care of your customer. **❞**
>
> **JONATHAN SALK**
> National Project Leader, NAR

to all members through the channel of their choice, which is the key to acceptance and participation. Functions in the dashboard will include a log of messages sent by association staff, alert messaging for emergencies and information on key issues.

9. Regional Realtor® Association Alliances

Proposed and to be developed by the Chicago, Mainstreet Organization, North Shore Barrington and Northwest Chicagoland Associations of Realtors®; they will be assisted by Jerry Matthews, Real Estate Advisor.

This is a formal, collaborative venture of Realtor® associations that primarily serve the Greater Chicago real estate market. Its focus will be information-sharing and the creation of an environment for a "community of trusted real estate advisors." Sharing staff talents would reduce the costs of duplicating staff and pass the savings on to their members, who will receive a broader scope of accurate information. The cooperative spirit between the associations would lead to faster resolutions of issues or concerns raised by members when working outside their local jurisdiction. The combined voice will lead to stronger support of legislative issues. Working together to protect and promote the Realtor® image in the media will heighten awareness of the value Realtors® provide.

10. Realtor® Finder

Proposed and to be developed by the Houston Association of Realtors®, Houston, Texas; they will be assisted by Jim Sherry of Innovative Solutions, Inc.

The Realtor® Finder system will allow consumers to identify Realtors® based on a number of performance criteria. The program starts with the theory that the "right" Realtor® is probably familiar with (and has been successful in) the immediate area where the consumer wants to buy or sell. In short, the Realtor® Finder system would provide consumers with the ability to select a Realtor® based on relevant and reliable transactional data from a "Realtor®-wise" resource. This system will promote agents based upon actual performance in both listing and selling. The system would show relevant agent market performance, knowledge and transactional expertise.

> ❝ NAR must be allowed to fail more and be allowed to take more risks and learn from it. ❞

 DALE STINTON
CEO, NAR

11. Realtor® Resume

Proposed and to be developed by the Bay East Association of Realtors® in California and Missoula Association of Realtors® in Montana; they will be assisted by Jeremy Conaway of RECON Intelligence Services.

Realtor® Resume will create an integrated customer relationship management tool that provides transparency for the broker and agent community.

It would track association member interactions and allow a broker/office manager to view a subset of the data. It would also establish data standards to allow agents to maintain a current resume of their education and professional training.

12. REWorx Dashboard

Proposed and to be developed by the West Volusia Associations of Realtors® in northwest Florida and the Northwest Mississippi Association of Realtors®; they will be assisted by Jeremy Conaway of RECON Intelligence Services.

REWorx dashboard will be a virtual instrument panel Realtors® use to manage the information and processes of their business. Members would log in to access all websites, transaction software, e-mail, social media, news feeds, market statistics and other information.

13. Sharing Landscapes

Proposed and to be tested by the Montana Association of Realtors®; they will be assisted by Kevin McQueen of Focus Forward Consulting.

This proposal will revolutionize an Association's service, especially in rural areas. To do this technology must be brought up to date for many local boards. This goal will be accomplished by providing basic satellite hookups, equipment and education that would allow members to more easily use social networking tools and other options to bring Montana Realtors® together. Information gained from discussion with stakeholders would be used to provide programs and services that better meet the needs of members, regardless of their location within the state.

14. Virtual Association of Realtors® Website

Proposed and to be developed by the Inland Gateway Association of Realtors®, Corona, California; they will be assisted by Stefan Swanepoel of RealSure, Inc.

This program would bridge the technology divide as agents get older and clients get younger. Similar to a virtual trade show, the Virtual Association of Realtors® would serve to attract both members and non-members to the online services. These would include podcasts, legislative briefings and consumer programs. The website experience will transport members to the next generation of online communication, interaction and customer service.

VALUE PROPOSITION

In considering this initiative process there are a number of bold questions that industry leaders and Realtors® are asking themselves and, therefore, we need to try and answer them. In a discussion with the NAR's National Project Manager, Jonathan Salk, we put those questions on the table.

Are these really game-changing ideas?

They may not all be in the same league but I believe that all those who submitted their ideas strongly believed that their ideas were important and could benefit their associations and perhaps others.

Implementation or the inability to implement has always been a challenge. Why will it be different now?

Yes, this is always an issue. The NAR has not indicated anything permanent yet, but I have to believe that if some of these projects prove to be a success, serious consideration would be given to implementing them on an ongoing or permanent basis. This is obviously my opinion and ultimately would be the decision of NAR leadership.

Will the average local association have the horsepower and resources to implement most of the ideas or is that just wishful thinking?

I think that if the Board of Directors of a local association feels strongly enough that their game changer idea needs to be implemented, they will

find the means to do it. This undoubtedly will require the allocation/re-allocation of resources, both financial and human.

The NAR said that, combined, the Game Changers offer a strategy to re-invent the local associations. Is that really valid? Do we have one strategic plan with a clear roadmap or do we really still only have a bunch of ideas – some good, some so-so?

While there were only 14 "winners," there are other great ideas in the mix of 200 including the runners-up and bright ideas. I think the NAR's comment is valid. Everyone will have their own opinion on what are the game changers and which ones are okay, but I believe that there are sufficient options and projects within the mix to allow an association to create a very powerful new strategic plan.

There were a total of another 200 or so proposals submitted and although all were not funded for development, the goal is that each of their almost 1,400+ Realtor® Associations will select from the list those programs that they can implement in their association.

 ## TAKE AWAY

Only time will tell which projects have legs and which don't. With that said, an initiative on a national scale to source over 200 ideas and then to beta test 14 of them with a budget is commendable.

Dale Stinton says that he looks forward to the day when a Realtor® member takes a survey and on all three levels — national, state and local — feels that he/she is getting good value for their dues. He is betting with significant confidence that these game-changing projects will collectively allow the NAR to drive change from the inside out, to change or to maintain (depending on where you stand) the NAR's relevancy in the future.

NAR's envisioned change will require acceptance and support across the board by all players. Whether this extraordinary approach will be successful and prove whether change can come from within is in the hands of the Realtor® members and will ultimately be determined by the surge or decline in the NAR membership.

Read All About It!

The End of Advertising as We Know It

OVERVIEW

CBS announced in December 2009 that it was cancelling the 54-year-old soap opera "As the World Turns." This followed the earlier announcement of the demise of its daytime staple, "Guiding Light," that had been on the air (radio and television) for 72 years.

December also saw the demise of *Editor & Publisher* Magazine, which had been around since 1854. It lays claim to being the chief chronicler of the American newspaper industry and has presided over the business for 125 years.

In a mid-2009 study, Anthea Stratigos, CEO of Outsell, Inc. (outselling.com), a media research and advisory outlet, predicted that $65 billion would be siphoned away from traditional advertising channels in 2009 and be spent on companies' own websites and Internet marketing.

There are no reliable industry-wide magazine ad revenue numbers that are publicly reported (for obvious reasons), but according to a report compiled by The Magazine Publishers of America's Publishers Information Bureau (PIB; magazine.org), automotive ads for the first six months of 2009 were down 21.3% and technology down 17.5%. Most of those to whom we spoke tended to agree that magazines are still doing better than newspapers.

> **"** Marketing is not about traffic, it's about conversion … [B]rokerages that decide to advertise online need a clear and defined game plan, and they had better understand their return on investment. **"**

TOM TOGNOLI
COO, Intero Real Estate Services

Newspaper and magazine readers are now primarily going to online resources to find what they want, a fact clearly reflected in the continuing decline of the newspaper industry.

SHIFT AWAY FROM NEWSPAPERS

Daily newspapers have been losing between 2% and 5% per year of their circulation base during the last 10 years. In 1940 there were 1,878 newspapers in the U.S. with a total circulation of 32.4 million. While the number of newspapers continued to decline — 1,611 in 1990 — their circulation increased: 62.6 million in 1990. But by 2008 the number of newspapers had dropped again by a little over 200 to 1,408 while circulation crashed down to 49.2 million.

> **"** If TV represented a body blow to the newspaper industry, the world wide web may prove to be the nail in the coffin. **"**

WHY ARE NEWSPAPERS DYING?
About.com

In the first half of 2009 alone another 105 newspapers closed their doors — 10,000 jobs were lost. Even among the leader board 23 of the top 25 newspapers suffered between 7% and 20% declines in circulation this year (the worst slump since the Depression), and advertising revenue could be down as much as a 30% for 2009 when all the data is finalized.

Four of the industry's big players represented 58% of the 105 closings in 2009:

- **Gannett Co. Inc. (7 failed newspapers)** saw its revenue fall 34.1% in the first quarter and it has laid off over 10,000 employees since 2007 — 22% of its labor force.

- **Gatehouse Media (8 failed newspapers)** saw its revenues decline 15% with losses of $3 million, resulting in a cut of 10.5% of its workforce in the first half of 2009; cutting the pay of another 7% to 15%.

- **Sun-Times Group (12 failed newspapers)**, owner of the Chicago Sun Times, filed for bankruptcy in April 2009 with losses exceeding $4.5 million per week between January and March.

- **The Tribune Company (34 failed newspapers)**, owner of the Los Angles Times and the Baltimore Sun, filed for bankruptcy in December 2008.

>  Shed traditional marketing messages. Engage and provide authentic value, expertise and relevance to the consumer. **"**
>
> **TERRI MURPHY**
> CIO, USLearning.com

Others of note:

- **The Journal Register Company** filed for bankruptcy in February with debt of $692 million.

- **Hearst Corporation** put the San Francisco Chronicle up for sale.

- **Christian Science Monitor** printed its last edition on April 3, 2009 and went online, publishing once a week.

- **E.W. Scripps** shut down the Albuquerque Tribune in February 2008 and the Rocky Mountain News in February 2009.

According to Pew Research (pewresearch.org), fewer than half of Americans (43%) say that if their local newspaper closed it would hurt their community "a lot," and even fewer (33%) say they would personally miss reading the paper. Over 68% indicated that they get their news from local television or television websites, 48% from print, 34% from radio and 31% from the Internet.

And one of the most critical statistics revealed that only 27% of Gen Y read a newspaper, compared with 55% of the Silent or Greatest Generation. As the consumers change so do their preferences, and the newspaper industry isn't the only one getting hit.

SHIFT AWAY FROM MAIL

The United States Postal Service (USPS, usps.com) estimated a $7 billion shortfall by the end of the fiscal year (September 2009) as a result of an 8.8% decline in revenue to $16.7 billion. The number of pieces of first class mail has steadily decreased and according to CEO Pat Donahoe, the USPS estimates a decline of 10 billion pieces in each of the next two years, dropping from a high of 213 billion pieces in 2006 to 170 billion in 2010. They are trying to cut costs in all areas to stop the bleeding: asking Congress to authorize reducing mail delivery to five days a week (approval unlikely), offering buyouts to 30,000 workers in 2010 to save $500 million and reducing

U.S. NEWSPAPER PRINT AD SALES QUARTERLY GROWTH

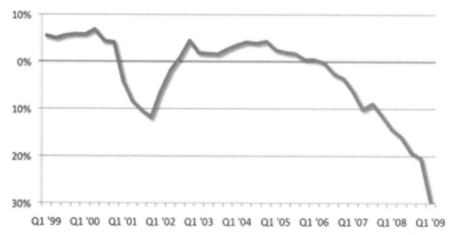

Source: Newspaper Association of America

the number of collection boxes across the country, of which in the past 20 years over 200,000 have vanished, more than the 175,000 that still remain.

But it's not just first class mail that is migrating to the Internet. The junk mail business is moving in that direction as well. Today there are 100 billion pieces of junk mail sent in the U.S. every year and 44% of it is discarded, unopened. Consumers respond to only 2% of all the junk mail sent and as a result one of the biggest producers of junk mail — the banking industry — has made getting out of the mail a high priority.

Consumers are changing and revenue from direct mail will fall from $48.7 billion in 2008 to $29.8 billion in 2013 — a decline of 39% — dropping it from the #1 ad revenue generator to #4, behind the Internet, broadcast TV and newspapers.

REAL ESTATE

In our *2006 Swanepoel TRENDS Report* we cautioned real estate brokers and agents to start to realign their marketing and advertising strategies. According to a Borrell Associates (borrellassociates.com) study in 2005 and again in

MEDIA USED BY REAL ESTATE AGENTS

	Media	2005	2009
1.	Newspapers	45.1%	28.8%
2.	Online	36.4%	55.4%
3.	Other print	7.8%	6.4%
4.	Direct Mail	5.0%	3.8%
5.	TV	2.9%	3.3%
6.	Yellow Pages	1.5%	1.0%
7.	Other	1.3%	1.3%

Source: Borrell Associates

2009, the media used by real estate agents for the most part remained unchanged, with the exception of newspapers and online. In 2005 the two platforms accounted for 81.5% of ad dollars spent. In 2009 that figure increased to 84.2%. The difference is that newspapers dropped with almost 40% and online rose with more than 40%.

In an AIM Group survey (aimgroup.com), it was reported that nearly six out of every ten real estate agents think newspaper advertising is useless.

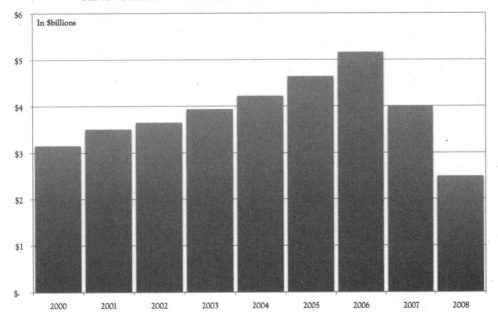

ANNUAL NEWSPAPER REAL ESTATE AD SPEND

In $billions

Source: Newspaper Association of America

Also in a report by the California Association of Realtors® (car.org) it was noted that only 13% of all home buyers looked at newspaper/magazine ads to search for a home, while 84% of home buyers used the Internet as a significant part of the home buying and selecting process.

Yet 30% of all agents still use print advertising on a regular basis and nearly 80% of all agents still buy print ads from time to time just to appease their clients. The real estate ad dollar decline according to the Newspaper Association of America (naa.org) rose from $3 billion in 2000 to a high of $5.2 billion in 2006 but collapsed to just $2.5 billion in 2008; back to '90s levels.

Nielsen News (nielsenratings.com) reported that the increase in visitors to the top U.S. real estate websites in July 2009 increased 11% month-over-month; 20.7 million visitors in June and 23.1 million in July. This was also reflected by ComScore Media Metrix (comscore.com). Realtor.com traffic was up 29% for the same period with overall time spent on the site up by 26%.

> **❝** Click-through is a poor measure of the value of web ads since it measures the alluring quality of your creative and not the ad's ability to deliver business. **❞**

 BORRELL ASSOCIATES

With a growing strength in online spending we project that by 2014 the distribution is expected to look something like this:

1. Online — 75%
2. Other Print — 10%
3. Newspapers — 5%
4. Direct Mail — 4%
5. TV/Cinema — 3%
6. Other — 3%

IMPACT OF THE INTERNET

Every day new technology emerges that enhances or expands our ability to communicate with others. Email has been the workhorse up to now but Social Media is making inroads as a major contender.

> **❝** Print and TV spending will go down to nearly zero and online spending starts to ramp up as the housing market starts to improve. **❞**

SPENCER RASCOFF
COO, Zillow.com

In 2008 advertisers spent $12.1 billion on email marketing — more than on display/banner or search advertising. Borrell Associates projects that online advertising formats, the preferred channel for all advertisers, will grow to $15.7 billion by 2013. Of that figure, approximately $2 billion will be allocated to local email advertising as companies abandon direct mail. As they do so they face the challenge of understanding the nuances of marketing in this segment.

This was also highlighted in a review by Borrell Associates of anticipated online budget changes in 2009 with 58.5% of respondents increasing their email budgets. It is also noteworthy that 43.9% are allocating more to Social Media (see Special Overview of Social Media). But the increase in email marketing comes with some significant consumer risks, as pointed out by Borrell, even from those who opt-in:

- 75% opt-out because they view the information as irrelevant;
- 73% opt-out because of too many emails received;
- 55% of opt-in email is deleted without being opened;
- 30% cease doing business with the company due to bad etiquette.

ALL LOCAL INTERACTIVE
AD SPENDING (projected in millions)

	Standard Format	Email/ Direct	Paid Search	Streaming A/V	U.S. Total
2013	$1,403	$940	$3,006	$2,110	$7,459
% Chg	(62.3%)	139.9%	34.9%	274.6%	7.9%

Source: Borrell Associates

And as these statistics indicate, consumers are already discounting email marketing in favor of pursuing online and digital markets directly.

With home Internet connection and home computer ownership figures now both approaching 70%, over 75% of adults report that they go online for various kinds of information; 26% report that they use the Internet a lot. Also it's no secret that Gen Y makes up a large part of that segment, the same segment that is poised to impact the real estate industry.

In attempting to reach this audience companies are spending heavily in the highly overcrowded Search Engine Marketing (SEM) marketplace with $11.5 billion spent in 2008. The magnetism of pay-per-click advertising is undeniable but the problem accompanying this growth is the lack of analytical tools that will accurately assess and recalibrate the effectiveness of ad spending.

The real estate industry is currently facing this problem in the broadest sense as it tries to determine the most cost effective and productive channels to deliver quality leads.

A projection of what and where small businesses in the U.S. are planning to expend ad dollars to reach this demographic is very telling. They clearly have grasped the message that consumers prefer an interactive format that is highly local in content. The format consists of: Standard (banners, pop-ups, etc.), Interactive Direct (email), Paid Search (Google, Yahoo!, etc.) and Streaming Audio/Video (online radio and TV).

Supporting these numbers is the estimate for local

Internet advertising at $22.99 billion in 2013; up from $12.89 billion in 2008 and $7.63 billion in 2007. Perhaps these numbers are also impacted by the results of a Harris Interactive survey (harrisinteractive.com) in 2009, which revealed that 65% of adults feel that they "could not live" without Internet access.

In addition, Booz Allen Hamilton (bah.com) in its *Marketing & Media Ecosystems 2010* survey reported the impact of advertising dollars moving into the digital segment. It revealed that 90% of those surveyed expect to spend more on digital advertising and 82% believe that consumer insights will become more important. This represents a reflection of the desire of the 18-to-49 age segment for more rich media ads. A survey by Dentsu Corp. (dentsu.com) revealed that 46.8% of those viewing a rich media ad "want to see it again" and 8.7% want to see it "very much."

> **44** A lot of Realtors® we talk to tell us the only reason they keep advertising is that their clients expect to see the ad in the paper. **77**

JIM TOWNSEND
Editorial Director, AIM Group

SO WHERE IS THE CONSUMER?

In a nutshell it all centers around two questions — where and how is the consumer looking for what they want?

Advertising objectives and goals by their very nature will vary from company to company and individual to individual. With that said, the *IPSOS Marketing & Media Survey* (ipsos.com) taken in January 2009 verified two key goals that have not changed. Over 63% of those interviewed indicated that New Customer Acquisition was their most important goal, with 32% stating it was important. This was closely followed by Increased Customer Retention with 42%, stating it was most important; Brand Awareness and Brand Favorability followed.

To achieve these goals the future allocation of advertising dollars is going to have to be a blend of the various options discussed in this trend: email, audio/video, SEM and Social Media, along with some offline expenditures. The successful advertising plan will have to be a hybrid or mashup of multiple channels if the consumer is to be reached and engaged.

That mashup cannot ignore the newspaper industry. Nielsen reported that in January 2009, there were over 75 million unique visitors to newspaper websites, an all-time high and a 12% increase over 2007. That means that over 44% of all active Internet users visited a newspaper website that month.

And one of the primary reasons for going in that direction is that in 2008 nearly equal percentages of Gen Y read a newspaper online and in print; 16% said they read only a print newspaper, or both the online and print versions, while 14% say they only read a newspaper online. There is a similar pattern for Gen X: 21% and 18% respectively. Even the Baby Boomers have increased their online readership over the past three years.

So, while there is a growing interest in interactive advertising it's very clear that the newspapers can't be avoided altogether. Alex Chang CEO of Roost (roost.com) recommends that agents breakdown their objectives they want to achieve in their online marketing, because social networking techniques that work well for branding, aren't as effective for client acquisition or listing promotion.

 TAKE AWAY

Advertising as we know it has changed — significantly.

The medium, the method and the message have all changed and it isn't finished yet. It's over as we know it, but the shift is still taking place.

Brokers and agents better quickly get their hands

around the new media platforms and determine how they work, which ones work (and which don't), which are most effective — from both a monetary and lead generating point of view — what the rules of engagement and participation are, how much to spend, and so on.

Changing the way you do business is always hard but understanding and changing at the same time is even more tricky.

Some of the long-standing questions you have always asked yourself are still valid (courtesy of *Marketing & Media Ecosystems 2010 Survey*):

- Are all elements of your advertising plan working?
- Are you getting the highest return for your investment?
- Do you have the right "look" for your market?
- Are you successfully branding your image?
- Are you addressing your Unique Selling Point (USP)?
- Which media fits your market and your approach to that market and are you properly leveraged?
- What form(s) of delivery is(are) most appropriate for your market?
- How much of your offline budget are you (should you be) shifting into other channels?

And the most important element:

- Prioritize your advertising efforts and commit to evaluating and changing it when and where required.

All of the above have a part to play in answering the key questions that will determine how effective your plan will be:

- Are you successfully engaging your customers where they are and are you relevant?
- Are you opening up and maintaining

communication with your customers?

- Are you utilizing emerging technologies?

- Are you measuring the success of your online marketing?

- Are you monetizing your Social Media efforts?

There are various trends this year that impact your company and personal business — read them all carefully.

Change by Design

Time to Grow Up

OVERVIEW

In today's rapidly changing economy there is more innovation and transformation than ever before. Many people are confused and waiting on someone else to take the initiative and step out with an answer — from the federal government on down.

Stop waiting. The time has come for you to take the necessary steps to change your business, your company and your career.

Real estate as a business has been changing for more than a decade now, but the pace is accelerating as we near the transformation years (other trends in this Report that clearly illustrate the transformation are Trends #5 and #6).

Innovation, education, re-positioning, re-structuring, implementation, etc. are all but a few of the keywords that need to fuel your daily thinking. The time has come to take the industry to the next level both structurally and professionally — and you, Mr. and Mrs. Realtor®, need to play your part.

> **❝** Real estate has never experienced such a "perfect storm" of events and factors, which have combined to force wrenching, dramatic changes upon a staid industry not accustomed to dealing with such seismic shifts. **❞**

MICHAEL MCCLURE
CEO, Professional One

Professionalism isn't a new term and it means different things to different people. But whatever it is or however we define it, it is a key building block as we move forward.

Let's first take a look at some of the primary drivers of the change. There are many elements that comprise this paradigm shift but three have become the core influence over the past few years: the economy, the consumer and technology.

THE ECONOMY

For the last few years the *Swanepoel TRENDS Report* has been discussing the concerns of irresponsible financial management and lending that now, as a result of reckless excesses in the industry, have tipped the economy upside down (see Economic Overview).

> **❝** This market will separate those who are skilled and true professionals from those who aren't, and will force the industry to set its standards higher. **❞**

MARTIN BOUMA
The Bouma Group, Keller Williams Realty

The current recession broadened widely in 2009 and has now affected almost 75% of all American adults. One-third of them have had someone in their household lose a job, had work hours or pay cut or had a mortgage foreclosed. One-fourth are concerned that someone in the household will lose their job and two-thirds have friends or relatives that have already suffered one of these events.

According to the latest UCLA Anderson Forecast (uclaforecast.com) this recession will be the longest one since World War II, with unemployment expected to top 10.5% in 2010. In addition, the next bump in the road is the resetting of approximately one million Adjustable Rate Mortgages (ARMs) over the next four years, 75% in 2010 and 2011. According to First American Core Logic (facorelogic.com) the peak will hit in August 2011.

According to the Congressional Budget Office (cbo.gov), America can anticipate federal deficits of $1.7 to $1.8 trillion for 2009; $1.4 trillion in 2010 and a minimum of $9.3 trillion between 2010 and 2019. Those estimates do not include the impact of a second stimulus, healthcare, cap and trade or the potential entry of inflation into the equation in 2011 as a result of all the borrowed (printed) money being thrown at the problems.

THE CONSUMER

It's no surprise to anyone that today's homebuyers and sellers have long since transcended the need for assistance in locating information. But what the consumer truly wants — and needs — can't be put into a system or a database. Consider the following responses from the California Association of Realtors® *Survey of California Home Buyers*, which explored what buyers want:

- A better understanding of the direction of the market;
- An improvement in the agent's negotiation skill; 82% were dissatisfied;
- More assistance in the mortgage approval process;
- A good understanding of purchasing distressed properties;
- A faster response time from the agent.

> 66 Our members have embraced the idea that feedback is beneficial to helping them become even better in their service to their clients … [O]ur Client Experience Rating allows those who actively use the program to set themselves apart from the rest. 99

BOB HALE
CEO, Houston Association of REALTORS®

Even though consumers had all the information, 54% of them still thought the information they gathered on the Internet was less useful than that provided by their real estate agent. But they are becoming harder to satisfy because they do have more information at their fingertips. At the same time the housing market dynamics have shifted from prior years when conditions were more favorable to sellers and now buyers realize that they have more power over the home-buying process than before. As a result, it is critical for agents to clearly understand the buyers' expectations and deliver accordingly, and that comes with a price.

The market and consumer knowledge/expectation are commanding more and more of the real estate agent's time and as a result, the business-as-usual approach has, for the most part, become obsolete. They have a good idea of what they want and where they want it. What they are looking for is trust, confidence, transparency, interpretation of information and additional services (mortgage, home warranty, inspection, etc.), all of which takes time (see table below).

In CAR's survey customer satisfaction was examined and the table on page 97 and graph on page 99 clearly reflect how the industry scored. Their overall dissatisfaction with real estate agents correlates directly with how they perceive the value they received; only 4% were satisfied with their agent and 12% with the value received.

Consumers are now looking much harder at "proof of experience" in the form of comments from past clients. In response, social networking channels have elevated the distribution of information to unimaginable levels. According to Quality Service Certification, Inc. (qualityservice.org), consumers are looking for information on the agent's past performance relative to professional accountability,

CUSTOMER SEARCHES

	Internet Buyers		Traditional Buyers	
Year	2006	2009	2006	2009
Weeks Searching Before Contacting Agent	4.8	7.0	1.7	4.5
Weeks Searching With Agent	2.2	10.0	7.1	11.6
Number of Home Viewed With Agent	6.7	13.6	15.4	25.0

Source: Cailfornia Association of Realtors®

reliability, consistency, responsiveness and overall service satisfaction. That demand, combined with the need for transparency, higher standards and better service is driving a need for agent ratings.

> **❝ I would like to say to my fellow agents: Realtors®! Educate yourselves, embrace this market and grow! ❞**

JIM SEXTON
Associate Broker, Russ Lyon Sotheby's International Realty

SOLUTIONS TO GROW UP

Normal is no longer normal. Your strategy has to change from a short term transactional one to a long term relational one. This will entail clearly defining the role you want to develop in the industry, considering your market and who is in that market. The generalist will never completely go away but it will be the specialist that emerges on top. For example, it is generally acknowledged that

50% of tomorrow's buyers will be either immigrants or minorities and a large percentage of them will be Gens X and Y; markets with widely varying wants and needs. Whatever your specific market, it's your market presence — your Unique Selling Point (USP) — that will set you apart from the competition. You need to understand it, develop it and perfect it. How you go about that is what this new mindset is all about. If you are still competing exclusively on the price and the commission you are ignoring what the consumer is really looking for — true value.

If Realtors® wish to improve their overall image with consumers and be seen as more professional there are a few very distinct actions they need to take:

- Improve the level of knowledge of existing agents and increase the entry level for new agents;
- Be willing to be let customers grade and rate the level and quality of their service;
- Utilize the new media frequented by the consumer to connect with them.

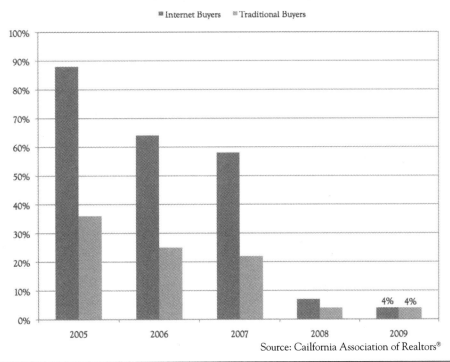

OVERALL SATISFACTION WITH AGENT USED
(Percent "Most Satisfied")

Source: Cailfornia Association of Realtors®

IMPROVEMENT OF KNOWLEDGE LEVELS

It is no longer about being licensed. That means nothing. It is no longer about being a member of the NAR. Few consumers understand the difference. It is no longer about the letters behind your name. The consumer doesn't care.

The consumer is looking for real knowledge, proven experience and professional quality service.

It's you, Mr. and Mrs. Realtor®, that must be willing to invest in yourself and make a commitment to identify the skills, knowledge and tools you need to enhance your ability to provide the professional quality service consumers are increasingly expecting, demanding.

> **"** The industry continues to be a complicated, dysfunctional compilation of individuals, companies and large corporations trying to figure out what the brokerage business should look like 3, 5 and 10 years from now. **"**

JOSE PEREZ
President, PCMS Consulting

The industry has for a long time convinced itself that a long list of designations behind one's name meant something to the consumer. But for the consumer it's not about a long list of letters they don't understand. It's about what you know and can apply to their specific needs.

Gen Y agents are especially adept at getting to the bottom line in this area. They focus on what they want and need in a given area to become successful and they do not want to have to wade through a great deal of class time to get it.

Professionals will turn more and more frequently to successful Realtors® and real estate professionals in their peer groups to selectively acquire the knowledge and skills they lack. This can of course be in a designation course, but today it can equally be obtained in an online webinar from a well organized traditional convention or from an "unconvention" such as RE BarCamp.

We used to call it education and training. Now its called knowledge and skills enhancement.

Forget CE. That's not knowledge, it's a requirement. Don't let the consumers be smarter than you are because they have spent hours surfing the web.

Ask yourself: Do I have all the specific knowledge that may be required for a specific task whether that's handling a short sale, a foreclosure, a luxury property, the staging of a home or a green transaction?

The time has come to focus on your knowledge, your skill set and the value you add to the consumer and not capitalized letters.

The future is still all about engaging the consumers at the point of their individual need and providing the appropriate service, just not the way it used to be done. The challenge is much greater today as the consumer now comes into the equation more prepared and fully armed with data. Therefore, professionals are going to have to become experts at quickly and efficiently determining consumer expectations while remaining flexible in the ways they meet those expectations.

RATED BY CONSUMERS

Consumers are looking more and more to the Internet to find out what the best hotels and restaurants are, to find information about various topics of interest and to rate service professionals. That now includes Realtors®. Websites with their only goal being to provide ratings and comments about Realtors®, such as OutrageousAgents.com, RealEstateRatingz.com and IncredibleAgents.com, have tried to provide a third-party platform for consumers, but according to web traffic measurement site Alexa.com none has garnered much attention from consumers.

Some Realtor® associations are considering developing their own Realtor® rating programs that will allow consumers to rate and review their Realtors® based on their personal experience. One example of where Realtor® ratings have been launched is at the Houston Association of Realtors® (har.com) with its Client Experience Rating Program. Always a pioneer and one to be watched by the virtue of its size — the largest local Realtor® association in the country — HAR began the program in March 2009 and has had more than 3,300 agents choose to participate as a way of differentiating themselves in their market.

According to HAR President and CEO Bob Hale the program was not without its initial skeptics so the association allowed its members to not make the results public so they would be the only ones to see the comments. Once the Realtors® saw the kind of positive feedback they were receiving there was a hope that they would then publish those ratings and comments. More than 26,000 surveys have been submitted and 47% of those have been answered, which is a very high percentage for an email survey.

Only a little more than 200 members have opted out of the program entirely.

> **&&** Key words for the real estate industry moving forward are: Lean, Clean and Green. **&&**
>
> **TAMI BONNELL**
> Founder & CEO, EXIT REALTY (USA)

One of the important aspects of the program is that it is all or nothing. Realtors® must either include all transactions in their rating or they are prevented from participating and cannot later jump back in. The integrity and transparency of the system must be there if the clients and the Realtors® are going to participate.

It is inevitable as the availability of information continues to expand and consumers exhibit the willingness to trust unknown raters on websites that Realtors® will be rated. It only becomes a question of whether they control their own destiny or allow

VALUE RECEIVED FOR WHAT YOU PAID
YOUR REAL ESTATE AGENT (Percent "Most Satisfied")

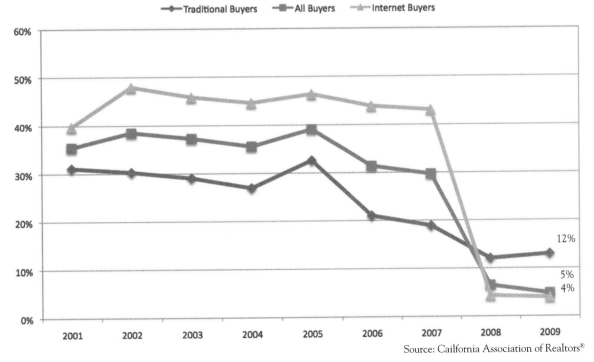

Source: Cailfornia Association of Realtors®

USING NEW MEDIA

The age profile of all homebuyers shows that the consumer is using the Internet, Search Engines, Consumer Facing websites, Social Media, etc., extensively in their search for real estate information in general and listing information in particular.

In most cases today consumers have already completed the majority of their basic homework on the Internet before making contact and most likely have a property or two in hand. What they want from their real estate professional is for them to provide, verify or validate the information, and that has become more important to them than the act of showing property.

> " We must increase entry level standards for real estate agents. We have made it too easy to gain entry into a profession that I have had so much respect for these past two decades. "

JERRY YOUNG
Broker Associate, Real Living Main Street Realty

Tomorrow's real estate professional must be prepared to quickly determine exactly what the consumers want, what they have, what they need and interpret that information for them in order to successfully counsel them on every aspect of the process — all in the manner and way they prefer to communicate. All of this is requiring agents to re-think how they've been operating and what they need to change in order to become tomorrow's real estate professional.

Are you perceived on Facebook and Twitter as the quality go-to real estate resource for your market?

Becoming the go-to resource for your market is a must, as everything is about hyperlocal content and who is the successful resource providing it. And

whether you like it or not, the emergence of Social Media and social networking has become the place where literally millions of consumers spend time.

There are new resources available to assist you in familiarizing yourself with the tools and the strategies used in this channel like the NAR's Web 2.0 & Social Media course and the 100-page *Swanepoel Social Media Report 2010* (published by the same company that publishes this Report). It all translates to the need for the real estate professional to become socially interactive with the consumer on multiple levels via multiple communication channels. Become, if you will, a media center for the consumer. A one-stop shop for everything local with timely, high-value content sourced from your valuable expertise and knowledge.

What it all comes down to is understanding that the Internet has both facilitated and complicated the process of gathering information and making decisions. Often the result has been too much information and a host of new questions. What the consumer wants and is willing to pay for is the professional's ability to sort that all out and help them make sound judgments. They want practical wisdom and the only way they can be persuaded that you possess that wisdom is through the valuable content and service you provide and how you provide it.

Consumers want one place to get all the information and one person to interpret it all and empower them to become an integral part of the transaction.

 TAKE AWAY

Professionalism has been defined in many ways, but they all have one thing in common: it's a mindset. It's not about what one does but rather how one does it. And that how has some general characteristics that are directly applicable to the real estate professional:

- **Professionals are driven by purpose, meaning and values.** They have an underlying love for what they do, which expresses itself in the quality of their work. They aspire to the highest goals of the profession.

- **Professionals constantly seek ways to improve.** No matter how good they are at what they do, they never rest on past accomplishments; they never stand still. They are always exploring new ways to ensure that the judgments they make are sound and based upon the practical wisdom they have acquired in the pursuit of their profession. They are always on the cutting edge and are willing to embrace new concepts and innovations that will help those they serve.

- **Professionals focus on what they do best.** They know their strengths and employ the systems and tools that will support them and keep them engaged in their primary task, using sound knowledge to provide sound advice.

- **Professionals focus on people.** They have developed excellent communication skills based upon a solid foundation of valuing the opinions of others and listening to them.

- **Professionals are consistent and committed.** They do what they promise irrespective of the personal cost. They understand that self-interest is subservient to the responsibility they have to those they serve.

However, what's important isn't the adoption of these individual characteristics, it's building the foundation of your personal business around them. Demonstrating the high level of honesty and integrity that accompany this foundation is the key to finding success. As a profession we can change, and we can do so by design. It's time that we take our industry to the next level.

Franchising Mix Modifies

Do You Want to Sit Up Front?

OVERVIEW

It's been almost 40 years since franchising entered the residential real estate industry and it has shaped the industry like few other concepts or strategies before or since. Its impact ranks with the MLS and the Internet as one of the top three game-changing strategies in real estate since World War II.

Today there are a growing number of agents questioning the value proposition of real estate franchising as they point to some of the older models that appear to offer little more than a brand. Even in today's online world the value of a brand is often questioned.

Looking back, one can view the first two decades of the franchising revolution as dominated by the speed and extent of its growth. Within a few years, we were not only introduced to new brands but they seemed to quickly enter almost every market.

During that time there were also some re-engineering phases as RE/MAX and Realty Executives offered up a different franchising business model. The majority of the large national real estate franchises, however, retained a very similar traditional model.

During last two decades, franchising has gone through a strong consolidation phase in which three groups have acquired over 10 significant real estate franchise brands. It started when Realogy acquired franchises (Century 21, Coldwell Banker and ERA Real Estate) and licensed the right to other established brands (Sotheby's and Better Homes & Gardens). Later Andrew Cimmerman amassed Realty World, Home Life and Red Carpet and recently Brookfield RPS became the owner of Royal LePage in Canada and GMAC Real Estate and Real Living in the U.S.

Then, during the mid 1990s, things seemed to change and a smorgasbord of hybrid models (Collaborative, Residual, Niche, etc.) began appearing and gaining traction. Today the number of real estate franchising brands and business models brokers can choose from has expanded significantly.

Brokers, of course, have always had the option of continuing to operate under their own brand and are generally referred to as Independents, but this is actually misleading as most franchisees are also independently owned and operated. And so, as we march into the next decade we are faced with the fact that selecting the right franchise has become a complicated process.

Choice is good but continuing to ride a non-stop carousel isn't.

> **“** There is an obvious need for consolidation in the number of franchisors just based on the size of the market. **”**
>
> **STEWART WILSON**
> Senior Vice President, Realogy

REAL ESTATE FRANCHISING CHANGES

Three large events, more than any others, have shaped real estate franchising in the past two decades:

- The roll-up of multiple franchise brands under one ownership;

- The evolution of the real estate business model;

- The adoption of franchising by historically independent regional brokers.

ROLL UP OF MULTIPLE BRANDS

When Hospitality Franchise Systems (HFS) — now Realogy (realogy.com) — entered the real estate franchise business in 1995 they changed the rules. First they acquired multiple brands, which was previously unheard of and not considered an option.

Second they started paying certain companies to join their franchise system. HFS theorized that by providing a "forgivable" loan to pay for conversion costs and future acquisitions it could convince brokers to affiliate with one of their brands.

Third they actually went out and acquired non-Realogy companies as well as franchisees within the stable and made them company-owned stores. Then they signed long-term (40-year) franchisee agreements with themselves, thereby solidifying a very strong base with the franchise.

> It's not enough to only be a well known franchise brand. You also have to be recognized for quality and results. **"**
>
> **HENRY WEBER**
> President/Regional Director, RE/MAX of New York, Inc.

The combination of all of these "new" initiatives allowed Realogy to undergo a period of unprecedented growth during their first decade in real estate.

EVOLUTION OF THE BUSINESS MODEL

The majority of real estate franchise business models have, for the most part, been largely centered on the traditional real estate brokerage model that was in play in the 1960s. Franchising added a nationally recognizable identity but generally did not create or enforce the standard business franchise practices found in most other industries where you are not only told where your specific location has to be, but also the look, method of operation, equipment to be used, product to be provided, etc. are all established by the franchisor. Think of franchises like McDonalds, Burger King and Jack in the Box – see one and you have seen them all. This ended up with the industry referring to the real estate franchising method as a "brand franchise."

Some real estate franchisors offer a selection of standard industry related tools and technology, relocation related services and sometimes leads generated from corporate marketing or websites. However, most do little more than encourage their franchisees to use the tools and systems, allowing

most to run their franchise without much interference from the franchisor as long as they are paying their franchisee fees and growing market share.

What has happened, however, is that every time someone comes up with a better way or a different approach to solving the real estate business model and a new franchise is usually born and offered up as the next big thing.

NEW BUSINESS MODELS

Not all new business models select franchising as a method to grow their company. Some have opted to remain in one city or region while those that do expand nationally can do so via various other methods such as operating their own company-owned offices, form an affiliate or business network or maybe even become a type of service provider.

Great new business model companies that are not discussed in this year's Report as they are not franchises include:

- Redfin
- ZipRealty
- @Properties
- Sawbuck Realty
- Estately.com

Along the way we have had many more failures than successes and many that have not really been able to expand beyond their first initial company owned prototype. But, a few have blossomed. We will be discussing the different franchising types a little later in this Trend.

The continued success of the franchising concept and the ease with which it allows brokers to rapidly expand, compared to opening and managing company-owned branches, started becoming attractive to many of the large regional brokers. By the late 1990s, anxious to expand their footprints, regional companies such as Weichert Realtors®, John L. Scott Real Estate, Crye Leike, Intero Real Estate, Howard Hanna and others jumped into franchising.

Most of these companies already operated a significant number of company owned branches, which they continue to operate today. By merely adding franchising as an adjunct to their existing business they could rapidly expand into other parts of the country they did not previously serve with their branch operations.

Increasingly it has become very difficult to compare or rank franchisor numbers — offices, branches, franchisees, sales volume, number of agents, etc. — as there are so many different combinations of ownership, and franchising mudding up numbers. With that said we have attempted to do so and offer up a ranking of the Top 20 largest franchisors later in this Trend.

“ Brokers need to change their business model... NOW. ”

SHERRY CHRIS
CEO, Better Homes & Gardens Real Estate

FRANCHISING QUO VADIS?

As in any type of franchising, success in real estate franchising is primarily about replicable implementation of a successful business model. In recent times it would seem that a large number of franchises have not fared well in that area and have lost their Unique Selling Point (USP) and/or their business model, while offering real estate brokers little more than a brand. However, there are some that offer a good, recognizable and, in some cases, a very desirable brand, one that is recognizable in the eyes of the consumer and therefore desirable in

the eyes of the real estate industry.

But that isn't enough. The downturn in the housing market has strongly underlined that you must have a successful business model as well. Due to the declining housing market and the subsequent decline in commissions and franchise fees, many franchisors have had to cut back on expenditures, staffing and thus the services offered to their franchisees. Many

“ [We are seeing] decline in the number of "big box" real estate office operations, which simply cannot survive given the high overhead levels typically associated with such large operations. ”

MICHAEL MCCLURE
CEO, Professional One

have cut back on their traditional sales teams that have been the bread and butter for most franchise networks, opting to rather focus on acquisitions and conversions. This has, in turn, led most franchisors to experience a contraction in the number of franchisees and/or agent count.

A franchise company's success (or failure) is, in the long term, dependent upon both its model standing the test of time and its systems supporting the local franchises in implementation of that model. For most, this has become difficult.

As such, there have been a disproportionate number of leading real estate brokerages (independent as well as franchisees) that stumbled during the last few years. In the previous *Swanepoel TRENDS Report* we detailed several that filed for bankruptcy, were closed or underwent a forced sale.

In 2008, there were a few very large and notable transactions including: Real Living's sale of Realty One (a Top 30 real estate company in the country at time of the sale) to Howard Hanna, the switch by Masiello Group (formerly the largest ERA franchise in the world) to the Better Homes and Gardens brand and the "forced sale" by GMAC of its national Real

FRANCHISING *Categories*

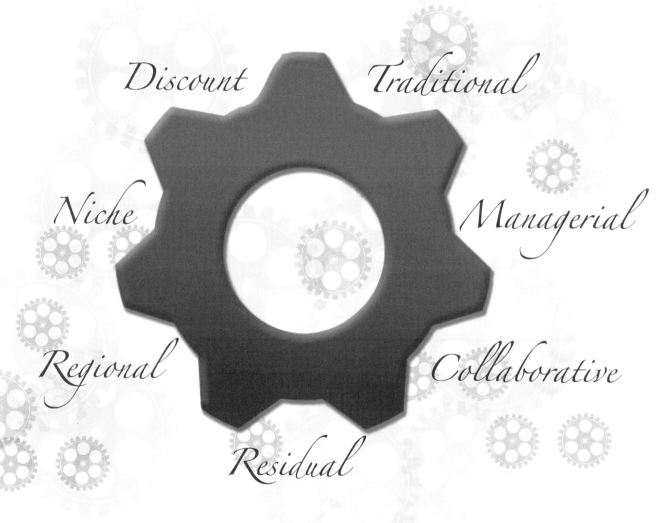

Estate Network (a top 10 national franchising brand) to Brookfield RPS in Canada.

And that trend continued in 2009.

- Century 21 Town and Country (the largest C21 franchise in the world at the time) filed for bankruptcy. They recently emerged from bankruptcy protection.

- Schweitzer, a huge Coldwell Banker franchise (one of the top 20 in the U.S.), was acquired by the much smaller, local, Birmingham-based Weir Manuel.

- Metro Brokers (the largest GMAC franchisee in the U.S.) moved across to become a Better Homes & Gardens franchise.

- Brookfield RPS in Canada struck again by acquiring Real Living (listed last year as the most promising new brand in real estate).

There are, of course, many more transactions — most smaller in size — but these illustrate that even the most prestigious and largest brokerage has not been immune from the affects of the failing housing market.

On the other hand, there was also good news and various interesting changes, restarts or start-ups.

- Real Living – The small new niche franchise was restructured and merged with GMAC Real Estate due to acquisition by Brookfield Property Services and is suddenly a whole new animal.

- Better Homes & Gardens – After a 10 year hiatus this brand returned to the residential real estate brokerage industry and as a national niche franchise with a fresh new, green image.

- Red Carpet – The return of an old/lost brand has come as a surprise to many. It was rolled out at the November 2009 NAR convention as a hybrid franchise offering rebates to agents.

- Oneir Realty – A new Florida-based franchise using multiple levels of income for sales associates (MLM concept) as their selling feature.

FRANCHISING CATEGORIES

Many of the franchise brands have become blended, looking very similar and losing ground and momentum in the process. Others again claim to be completely unique while fundamentally they are not that much different. Many are still relatively small and their path going forward has not yet been exactly determined.

> **"** This has been make-or-break time for real estate franchises. They must invest in staff and resources to help their affiliates stay in business and then build when others are declining. That's the real franchise opportunity — to add substance underneath the colorful veneer. **"**

MARTY RUETER
President, Weichert Real Estate Affiliates, Inc.

While it is extremely difficult to classify franchising companies into specific categories, here is how we believe they currently stack up:

1. Traditional
2. Managerial
3. Collaborative
4. Residual
5. Regional
6. Niche
7. Discount

1. **Traditional Franchises** use a selection and a sliding scale of compensation plans to pay the agent that earned the commission. Examples include:

   - Coldwell Banker
   - Century 21
   - ERA Real Estate
   - Prudential Real Estate Affiliates
   - Weichert Realtors®

2. **Managerial Franchises** charge a flat monthly administrative or management fee to their

Real Estate Franchises
TOP 20 for 2009

Based on USA agent count at 12/31/09 – adjusted for major 2009 mergers and acquisitions and decline in agents
Source: Real Trends 500 Survey, RIS Media Power Broker Survey, RealSure Top Franchises Survey,
Realtor® Magazine Survey, Inman News and various interviews with CEOs.

Agent Range	Ranking	Name of Franchise
75k +	1	Century 21
	2	Coldwell Banker
	3	Keller Williams
50-75k	4	RE/MAX
	5	Prudential
25-50k	6	ERA
	7	EXIT
10-25k	8	Weichert Realtors®
	9	Realty Executives
	10	Real Living (GMAC)
5-10k	11	Sotheby's
	12	Windemere
	13	Realty World
< 5k	14	Better Homes & Gardens
	15	United County
	16	John L Scott
	17	Assist-2-Sell
	18	Crye-Leike
	19	Avalar
	20	HomeSmart

sales associates for the use of services rendered. Examples include:

- RE/MAX
- Realty Executives

3. **Collaborative Franchises** share net profits based on profitability of each market center. Examples include:

- Keller Williams Realty

4. **Residual Type Franchises** share revenue on closed transactions across multiple levels of sales associates. Examples include:

- EXIT Realty
- Avalar Real Estate
- Professional One
- Oneir Realty

5. **Regional Franchises** usually operate as a Traditional Model although they operate only in a specific geographical region of the country.

- John L Scott Real Estate (North-West)
- Windermere Real Estate (West)
- Crye-Leike Realtors® (Mid-South)

> **❝** I don't think a pure brokerage play as business strategy is a viable play in this economy or going forward. **❞**

RON PELTIER
President & CEO, HomeServices of America

6. **Niche Franchises** focus predominantly on a specific niche. Examples include:

- United Country (Country Homes, Farms & Ranches)
- Sotheby's International Realty (Very High End Homes)
- Casa Latino (Hispanic Market)
- Engel & Vöelkers (Luxury Homes and Boats)

7. **Discount Franchises** offer some form of reduced real estate fee or rebate to buyers/sellers. Examples include:

- Assist-2-Sell
- Home Life

FIVE MOST EXCITING FRANCHISES

It's no secret that the number of home sales is far lower than it was three years ago and, therefore, it is not surprising that most franchises have contracted in number of offices and/or agent count. Yet, at the same time, we have significantly more franchise options than ever before.

> **❝** In cases where their franchising is faltering, the culprit is most often that the models of the real estate company are not suited for these times. **❞**
>
> **BRYON ELLINGTON**
> Chief Products Officer, Keller Williams Realty

In the opinion of many brokers and agents, many of the "older" franchises (majority of the Top 10 are in the 30+ years category) have become stale or they have saturated the market to such an extent that growth for even ambitious franchise owners can be limited. Consequently there appears to be a large interest in new innovative business models, highly visible and well established brands with the consumer, the collaborative and profit sharing model and the well known brands that are new to real estate and, therefore, still have many open markets.

Despite the slowing in the housing market the following five national franchises are, in our opinion (at least for now), the top five brands that have the most potential for success in the future. We have listed them in alphabetical order:

- **Better Homes & Gardens Real Estate** – This much smaller and relatively new but well known brand has a zealous following and is, for various reasons, well positioned to grow disproportionately over the next few years. With the resources of Realogy behind it, BH&G has become an attractive alternative for frustrated franchisees that, for whatever reason, have out grown their existing brand. Validating this is the fact BH&G has expanded into 13 states with over 5,000 agents in approximately 18 months.

- **Coldwell Banker Real Estate** – Realogy has always been very strong in the mergers and acquisitions (M&A) arena through their subsidiary NRT, Inc., and Coldwell Banker has usually been the brand that benefitted from most of these acquisitions. With Realogy continuing this strategy and focusing on acquiring some large companies to roll into their network, this 103-year-old brand has proven to be one of the most successful and enduring of all time.

- **Keller Williams Realty** – In his book *SHIFT*, Gary Keller wrote: "You can't build a business by cutting back, but you can find your profit and save it." By sharing profits, Keller Williams has allowed real estate professionals to earn additional income beyond their most recent sale and to a certain extent ride out the seasonality and cycles of personal sales. This, coupled with a unique "team culture," has propelled Keller Williams into being ranked the #1 franchise by both *Entrepreneur Magazine* and a national survey among 10,000 agents undertaken by RealSure in December 2009.

> **"** We feel our brand recognition is so high because of our extensive advertising campaign. **"**

MARGARET KELLY
CEO, RE/MAX International

- **RE/MAX International** – Although 2009 was a difficult year for RE/MAX owners on numerous fronts, the brand awareness continued to soar. This was especially true on the global front where

they signed contracts in 10 new countries and on the airwaves where Nielsen Media Research showed RE/MAX holding 99.9% of the national share of voice in television advertising. According to RISMedia and REAL Trends surveys, RE/MAX Sales Associates also remain the most productive in transaction sides and dollar volume. The November 2009 rankings by Hitwise (hitwise.com) placed remax.com as the 10th largest website in the real estate category based on market share, ahead of all other real estate franchisors.

- **Sotheby's International** – While much smaller than Coldwell Banker or Keller Williams, Sotheby's has however claimed the very respected position of the most sought after luxury homes brand in real estate. Their very high cache value has been successfully transferred from their global high-end auctioneering brand and offers brokers and agents a leg up in positioning themselves above many other more traditional real estate brands.

☑ TAKE AWAY

Few real estate franchise operations have been spared from the decline of the real estate brokerage industry over the past few years. This has caused many of them to cut back on the services offered, resulting in franchisees being touched much less than they were in the past and causing many to question, legitimately or not, why they are still paying franchise fees.

With many brokerage companies themselves in full survival mode the additional franchise fee (as high as 6%) is often brought into question, thus resulting in accelerating consolidations, acquisitions by the franchisor or franchisees leaving when their contracts come up for renewal.

Furthermore, according to a survey undertaken by Better Homes & Gardens, the average size of a real estate office today is around 127 square feet per agent. This is too large and one of the primary reasons that brokerages are unprofitable. BH&G feels that today an average allocation of 50 square feet per agent is more suitable and will actually, over the course of the next few years, decline to 25 square feet.

Many residential brokers and agents believe that they don't need a brand and that the Internet and Social Media have made the franchise obsolete. This is clearly not the case. Many brokers and agents want or need a brand while others want and need different kinds and levels of support. That will continue to create opportunities for different franchisors to attract different brokers and agents to their fold.

But it would seem that the years of offering little or no service are rapidly disappearing and those franchisors wishing to be successful in the future will have to offer considerably more than just a brand. Franchisors must be able to justify the initial and ongoing fees by providing real value to their franchisees. Some are already doing that and will continue to grow as outlined in this Trend.

Those that are unable to reinvent themselves or offer value will decline into obscurity and/or become a casualty or an acquisition as the industry consolidates.

Time for Market Fundamentals

Is the Tax Credit All It's Supposed to Be?

OVERVIEW

The economic crisis has been laid at the feet of many parties and how we got there and what caused it has been the fodder for countless arguments for months. While not everyone agrees on those issues, they are generally in agreement that it is going to take a revitalized and healthy housing market to turn things around. But in light of tighter credit standards, falling house prices and an economy in recession that goal appeared to be out of the question in the near term. So in an effort to jumpstart the housing market, the federal government took a first step with its First-Time Homebuyer Credit (FTHBC), details on the opposite page.

The government, supported by the NAR and many in the industry, believes that the tax credit is working and is the stimulus that will entice first-time buyers sitting on the sideline to make the move into the market. When the credit was due to expire last fall the NAR supported the extension proposed by Washington under the Worker, Homeownership and Business Assistance Act of 2009 that was signed by the President on November 6th. In the process of lobbying for that extension and the discussion of the results to date, two very distinct camps emerged: those who believe the program is the key to turning the market around and those who believe it is ineffective and will not help.

Is the FTHBC a key to turning the market around? We'll start by looking at the results so far.

> **"** I think we should be cautious about confusing economic activity with economic improvement. A program that largely re-shuffles houses (between homeowners or from renters to buyers) will generate lots of activity, but will not help housing fundamentals. **"**

DR. TED GAYER
Co-Director Economic Studies, The Brookings Institution

REPORT CARD

In judging how well the FTHBC has done to date we'll first look at the results as viewed by the NAR and the federal government and then how it is viewed by others.

HOUSING WEALTH

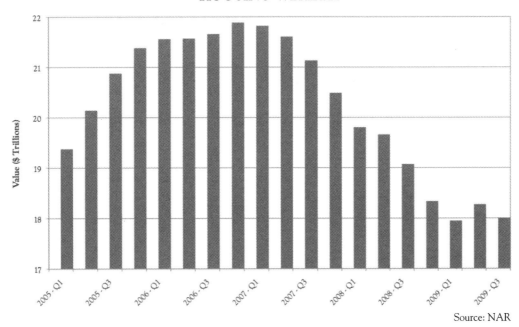

Source: NAR

ELIGIBILITY REQUIREMENTS FOR THE FIRST-TIME HOMEBUYERS CREDIT	2008 FTHBC	2009 FTHBC
Date of purchase must be between April 9, 2008 and June 30, 2009	x	
Date of purchase must be between January 1, 2009 and November 30, 2009		x
Home must be personal residence(1)	x	x
Taxpayer must have no prior homeownership within the past 3 years	x	x
Home cannot be a gift or inheritance	x	x
Home cannot be acquired from a relative	x	x
Home must be located in the United States	x	x
Single filers: Modified adjusted gross income (MAGI)(2) must be less than $95,000 Between $75,000 and $95,000 the credit phases out	x	x
Married filing jointly filers: MAGI must be less than $170,000 Between $150,000 and $170,000 the credit phases out	x	x
Cannot claim the FTHBC in both 2008 and 2009	x	x
Taxpayer cannot be a non-resident alien	x	x
Taxpayer must not be or must not have been eligible to claim the District of Columbia homebuyer credit for any year	x	
Home financing cannot come from tax-exempt mortgage revenue bonds	x	
15 year payback provision; accelerated if home is sold or is no longer the personal residence	x	
Recapture provision if the house is resold or ceases to be the primary residence within 3 years; limited to the amount of the gain		x

Source: U.S. Government Accountability Office, October 22, 2009

(1)A principle residence is the main home a taxpayer lives in most of the time. It can be a house, houseboat, housetrailer, cooperative apartment, condominium or other type of residence.

(2)MAGI is modified adjusted gross income (AGI), as figured on an income tax return, plus various amounts excluded from the income tax return, such as some types of foreign income that would have to be added to AGI to yield MAGI

Extension of the 2009 Tax Credit (November 2009)

First-Time Homebuyers
The term of the 2009 First-Time Homebuyer tax credit was extended to April 30, 2010 for homes under contract by April 30, 2010 and close escrow by June 30, 2010 that are their primary residence.
- The income limits were raised to $125,000 for single filers and $225,000 for joint filers.
- The purchase price of the home cannot exceed $800,000.
- The homebuyer must submit a properly executed copy of the home purchase settlement statement with the tax return when claiming the tax credit.

Existing Homebuyers
The credit was extended to existing homebuyers in the amount of 10% of the purchase price; up to $6,500. They must have lived in the home for five consecutive years of the past eight years.
- The home must be their primary residence.
- The income limits are $125,000 for single filers and $225,000 for joint filers.
- The purchase price of the home cannot exceed $800,000.
- Homebuyer must submit a properly executed copy of the home purchase settlement statement with the tax return when claiming the tax credit.

For members of the Armed Forces deployed on duty outside the United States, the tax credits are extended to May 1, 2011 (must close before July 1, 2011) Military homebuyers must be deployed outside the U.S. for at least 90 days between Dec 31, 2008 and May 1, 2010.

NAR

The NAR reports that a combined 1.2 million transactions (400,000 resale and 800,000 new) were the direct result of the credit since its inception, contributing approximately $22 billion to the general economy. It is their estimate that two million people will take advantage of the credit in 2009. Dr. Lawrence Yun, NAR Chief Economist, estimates that in 2010 existing home sales will enjoy a 15% increase and that home prices will rise from 3% to 5% during the same period. Yet he voiced some concern in December 2009 at the Triple Play Realtors® Convention in delivering his *Housing Market Trends & Outlook* presentation. Yun questioned whether or not the FTHBC is, in effect, a real tax credit or something else altogether. It's his opinion that the $8,000 is really not a credit in the truest sense, but rather a drop in the price of the house. While that makes no difference to the buyer, for the housing market as a whole it should be a major concern.

> 66 It [First-Time Tax Credit] will help chip away at inventory levels, stabilize prices and spur sale activity. 77

RICHARD A. SMITH
CEO, Realogy

Utilizing an average selling price of $200,000, Yun pointed out that the $8,000 tax credit should also be viewed as a 4% decline in value. Taking that premise to its conclusion translates the results into a potential destruction of housing wealth in the amount of an additional $730 billion to be added to the $4 trillion already lost from housing peak late in 2006.

In support of the NAR, the California Association of Realtors® (car.org) reported that for 75% of first-time homebuyers in California the tax credit was very important and more than 40% would not have been able to buy without it. Others in the industry suggest that the tax credit was a big assist in selling the short sale inventory prior to the pre-extension deadline of November 30, 2009.

NAR's 2010 President-Elect Ron Phipps suggested that if just 5% of the current 16 million renters who could purchase a home were convinced to do so by the tax credit it would result in 800,000 additional home sales — sales that he said would generate $60,000 in additional economic activity per sale.

The federal government examined the results and their report reveals more detail on the success to date.

THE FEDERAL GOVERNMENT

The Treasury Inspector General for Tax Administration (treas.gov/tigta) estimates that the number of transactions by the end of 2009 will be 1.4 million, less 94,000 that will not be deemed first-time homebuyers. Congress had allocated $13.6 billion to the program in anticipation of achieving two million home purchases; $6,800 per transaction.

In testimony before the House of Representatives on October 22, 2009, James R. White, Director Strategic Issues for the United States Government Accountability Office (GAO; gao.gov), reported the following interim results.

TAXPAYERS CLAIMING THE FTHBC IN 2008 AND 2009

	2008	2009	Total
Number of taxpayers claiming the FTHBC	1,041,361	385,193	1,426,554
Dollar amount of credit claimed (billions)	$7.108	$2.89	$9.998

Source: IRS data as of August 22, 2009

When the GAO reviewed the claims in relationship to Adjusted Gross Income (AGI), the report revealed that the majority of claims were filed by taxpayers with AGIs of less than $50,000; especially those under $25,000 (See table below). In the process the GAO identified the top ten states claiming the tax credit (See table on opposite page).

But while the NAR and the government score the results well, there are those who have not graded it so generously. To them, it has not been so much about the numbers as it has been about the effective cost.

THE QUESTION OF COST

There are many critics of the tax credit that question how much value it really delivers for the cost, suggesting that the actual cost will be $15 billion (twice what Congress budgeted), $43,000 per homebuyer that would not have bought a house without the credit. That brings up their real concern — the loss of tax revenue in a period of increased governmental spending.

Lost Tax Revenue

Shaun Donovan, the secretary of the Department of Housing and Urban Development (hud.gov), in expressing doubt over the need to extend the tax credit suggested in testimony before the Senate that while it's clear the credit benefited the industry, the real issue is the cost to the government in lost tax revenue. He is not alone in his opinion.

Many inside and outside the industry are of the

opinion that most of the homes purchased credited to the tax credit would have been made anyway. According to Andrew Jakabovics, associate director for housing and economics at the Center for American Progress (americanprogress.org): "In about four out of five cases, the tax credit went to people who would have bought a home anyway. So that means the real cost of getting that one extra buyer into the market is five times $8,000 — about $40,000." Even the NAR reported that only 350,000 of the two million new homebuyers say they would not have bought a house without the tax credit.

> " Real estate is a cyclical business so values go up and go down. Time heals all problems of real estate; it's just that most people run out of time. "
>
> **EARL LEE**
> President, Prudential Real Estate and Relocations

In its comments the GAO noted several challenges the IRS faces including verification that all claims are valid first-time homebuyers and the ultimate collection of up to $7 billion in repayments due under the terms of the 2008 credit. One of the key issues is the fact that the IRS did not require validating documentation from the taxpayer or any third-party source. The question on the table now is how much fraud has actually been committed utilizing the credit.

TAXPAYERS WHO CLAIMED FTHBC 2008/09 COMBINED COMPARED TO ALL 2007 TAXPAYERS

	0 or Less	$1 to $25,000	$25,001 to $50,000	$50,001 to $75,000	$75,001 to $100,000	$100,000+	Total
Number FTHBC claims	25,200	2645,283	543,996	352,474	152,054	87,547	1,426,554
Percentage of total FTHBC claims	2%	19%	38%	25%	11%	6%	100%
Percentage of total 2007 taxpayers	1%	40%	24%	14%	8%	13%	100%

Source: IRS data as of August 22, 2009

Fraud

The Inspector General of The Treasury Department (TIGTA, ustreas.gov) disclosed that as of September 30, 2009, the IRS had identified 167 suspected criminal schemes and opened nearly 107,000 examinations of potential civil violations; 8% of the 1.4 million home sales that have claimed the credit. In a separate report TIGTA found that 19,351 2008 tax returns claims were made for homes that had not been purchased, totaling $139,555,174 inappropriate claims. Another $500 million claims by some 74,000 taxpayers were made where there were indications of prior homeownership. They also reported that 582 taxpayers under 18 years of age claimed nearly $4 million; the youngest was four years old.

One In - One Out

One issue that has generated a great deal of concern is the extension of the $6,500 tax credit to existing homeowners. While it is a bonus to the home buyer it does virtually nothing to reduce the housing inventory. According to Harvard economics professor Dr. Edward L. Glaeser: "A buyers' credit that goes to everyone creates a strong incentive for purely mindless house swapping." He further concluded that basic economics suggests that a policy that provided equal incentives to buy and sell will do little to increase housing prices.

Stan Humphries, Chief Economist for Zillow (zillow. com), noted that four out of five sales of houses to first-time homebuyers would occur regardless of the tax credit. He determined that the extension of the credit would generate an incremental 334,000 sales (sales not occurring without the credit) at a cost of $14.86 billion, $44,491 per house. The government · estimates the extension will cost $10.8 billion in lost tax revenue. But more problematic he notes is the fact that while the credit may generate 300,000+ plus sales, there are almost three million homes in the foreclosure pipeline: "it's like draining your bathtub with a spoon while leaving the faucet running."

RENTERS TO OWNERS

Another area of concern stems from the fact that most first-time homebuyers come out of the rental market, and a home purchase results in an apartment vacancy. According to MarketWatch (marketwatch.com), in the second quarter of 2009 there were a record 4.4 million apartment vacancies in the U.S. (10.6% of all

STATE-LEVEL FTHBC CLAIMS FOR 2008/09

Rank	State	Filers Claiming Credit	Total Dollars Claimed (Millions)
1	Nevada	20,177	$146.370
2	Utah	17,568	$129.687
3	Arizona	38,130	$275.500
4	Florida	105,865	$770.496
5	Tennessee	35,836	$256.185
6	Georgia	55,840	$398.493
7	Nebraska	10.149	$70.894
8	Idaho	8,525	$61.972
9	Minnesota	28,780	$200.222
10	Michigan	55,116	$362.430

Source: U.S. Accoountability Office

units), and there were 1.9 million vacant owner-occupied dwellings. They believe that the housing problem in America isn't that home prices are falling; it's that there are so many vacancies that prices must fall.

MarketWatch suggests that the correct solution to this problem is to create new households, not shuffle them from one form of housing to another, moving young adults out of their parents' basements and into apartments. Their other concern is that since the credit can be monetized to get into a government-subsidized FHA loan and used as a down payment, it encourages buyers to put less of their own money into the purchase; leading to more defaults in the future.

> ❝ We in real estate experience a recession every seven years on average, twelve of them since 1929. Each downturn is different in nature due to compounding economic factors of the time, but the effect is the same for our industry. ❞

BOB MCKINNON
Senior Regional Consultant, EXIT Realty

Ted Gayer, Co-Director, Economic Studies, The Brookings Institution (brookings.edu) agrees: "… [M]ost of the new home sales just result in moving renters to owners, which does not absorb the excess supply of houses. The core of our weak housing market is that the housing bubble led to too many homes being built, and the recession has led to a decline in household formation. By moving renters into owners, the tax credit does not address either of these causes." Gayer also said in an interview with Politico (politico.com), that we should be cautious about confusing economic activity with economic improvement; a program that largely re-shuffles houses between homeowners or from renters to buyers will generate lots of activity, but will not help housing fundamentals. All of which raises a lot of questions that are without answers at the present time.

AN UNCERTAIN TOMORROW

Both sides of the FTHBC issue agree that it's clear the real estate industry and a number of homebuyers have definitely benefitted from the program. On the other hand, they do not agree on just how much this has cost and will cost the American taxpayer in the future. That jury is still out and may not come in with a verdict until well into 2011.

That fits with the concern of this Report — will the first-time homebuyer tax credit be part of the solution to the country's economic problems or just contribute to it? We are putting a lot of taxpayer money into a program that isn't delivering a large number of home purchases and may not be addressing the critical issue of an excess supply of homes. Of further concern is the fact that historically the majority of temporary governmental programs have a habit of being extended. In November 2009 the industry made its case to have the credit extended to avoid a slowdown in the market; the strong potential exists for that to happen again in June 2010.

> ❝ [First-Time Tax Credit] will not turn things around … [G]iven the economy it will only push a precious few first-time homebuyers over the edge right now. ❞

JARED BERNSTEIN
Economic Policy Institute

And one only needs to look back at the Cash-For-Clunkers program as an example of government programs failing to deliver what they promised. It is now commonly accepted that the program predominately benefited those who were planning on buying a car already. In addition, upon completion of the program, new car sales slumped once again. Fortunately it was not extended, as many in Congress were lobbying. It would appear that we may be headed down that same road with the FTHBC.

TAKE AWAY

Tax expenditures are not a free lunch. Everything spent on these programs will ultimately have to be paid for sooner or later through higher taxes. With all the government programs being established to support multiple interests the pending tax burden is going through the roof. The bottom line for real estate, just as it is for every other industry, is to deal with the issue based on solid market fundamentals if it is going to stand on its own two feet once again. The housing market must be allowed to establish a market-based solution, prices based upon the homebuyers' true financial capabilities as measured by reasonable credit standards. Not a solution that is based on a continued government subsidy.

> Fifty-five percent of loan modifications have failed after six months because jobs are not being created and homewoners are losing the jobs they have. **"**

JIM GILLESPIE
President & CEO, Coldwell Banker Real Estate

The housing market will ultimately have to make its own correction, but that will not happen until a very critical piece of the puzzle gets put into place; employment. If the government will establish the unemployment issue as its number-one priority and channel its efforts into resolving that problem, then the country will begin to see progress in a number of areas, real estate being one. While the issues of healthcare and energy are important, they do not supersede the issue of getting America back to work. We cannot continue down the path we have been on for the past few years of depending upon the government to hold the market in place. If we get Americans back to work, then more people will be able to qualify for homeownership on solid financial terms. Then and only then we will begin to whittle away at the excess housing problem. The true bottom of the market must be established, and then we can begin a solid climb out the other side.

The status quo will not resolve the problems. Continuing to subsidize the problem by extending the tax credit again and again in the face of the huge number of ARMs resetting in 2010 and 2011 may prove to be very problematic, and borrowing and printing money to fund the cost is not the answer either. Combining all of this with increasing interest rates by the Fed and the increased tax burden the government programs create and you have the recipe for inflation. It is a recipe that may prevent us from getting a healthy housing industry that we need to get us back into a growing economy — a growing economy that will cure a lot of ills.

Protecting Your #1 Asset

Mission Statement: To Organize All Real Estate Data

OVERVIEW

For a decade and a half, starting with *Real Estate Confronts Realty* in 1997, the 10 subsequent books and white papers in the Real Estate confronts series and in the five annual *Swanepoel TRENDS Reports* since 2006, we have been writing about the importance of real estate information and data.

Often the comparison has been made that real estate agents are analogous to Google — they also own no gold mine or manufacturing plant but have the ability to sort through lots of data. In the case of real estate agents it's sorting through listings for sale and assisting buyers in determining the properties that meet their particular needs by providing them with the desired results through interpretation, guidance and counseling.

Information is at the very core of Google's astronomical rise to global dominance. Taking real estate data and mixing it with an agents knowledge of neighborhoods and current sales data in particular is at the very core of being an effective, successful real estate professional.

The access to quality data and the ability to analyze interpret and offer up that data more efficiently than anyone or anything else sets the professional apart. Sitting in the center of one of the largest, most exciting and most active industries that is at the very core of our economic system.

We live in it, work in it, drive on it and play on it. It's a matter of fact that there is very little we do that doesn't, in some way, involve real estate. Without data — quality real-time data — real estate agents may very well consider their job, their profession, a threatened species.

Therefore, the single most important task at hand is to store, protect and control real estate's most valuable asset – the property data. Luckily, in 2009 someone stepped up to do just that. Let's explain in more detail.

BACKGROUND

During the early 1990s businesses across the U.S. began to realize the influence and potential impact the Internet was poised to have on the way products and services were marketed, purchased and delivered. The "experts" were predicting that many service providers would disappear as consumers were able to obtain the same services themselves through the Internet at a lower or discounted price. Real estate agents were frequently mentioned as service providers at substantial risk of seeing their business dramatically impacted by new Internet ventures. Access to an aggregated database of properties listed for sale, which had only been available to Realtors® through membership in a Multiple Listing Service (MLS), was the primary issue cited. Consumers wanted the ability to search for available properties themselves without having to contact a Realtor®.

> **"** As long as I am at the head of NAR, there will be no attempt to generate revenue from RPR. It is the ultimate member benefit. **"**
>
> **DALE STINTON**
> CEO, NAR

In 1992 the National Association of Realtors®, while recognizing the potential threat to Realtors® should the above services be created, saw the opportunity to take a leading role in providing that information. This decision led to the development of Realtor.com, which today is a leading consumer destination for properties for sale.

The development and implementation of Realtor.com was anything but smooth. The industry naysayers at the time said the NAR was trying to take over the MLS and that the NAR had no business attempting to become involved with a commercially run Internet business. Many significant problems were encountered along the way, but in the final analysis, had the NAR not taken the chance, the real estate profession and the Realtors® role in the transaction would most likely have been negatively impacted.

THE CHALLENGE AND SOLUTION

Over the last decade consumers have increasingly gained online access to more robust and detailed real property-related information. Ironically, although Realtors® have access to the same information through the MLS, it is often not as well displayed or integrated.

As a result the perception that consumers need to contact their local Realtor® if they want to know more about individual properties, communities, local trends, regulations and other factors related to local real estate is changing. The need for the Realtor® is once again being challenged.

> " I think RPR will be a force in 2010. For good or for evil remains to be decided. "

ROBERT DRUMMER
Agent, Keller Williams Realty

In finding a solution, creating a robust property-centric national library or archive that has useful information on virtually every property in the U.S. is good place to start. If this collective knowledge could be organized and archived in a single industry-sponsored and operated database, real estate agents could share their expertise and unique knowledge at the neighborhood level and leverage their collective experience. For their customers it will mean broader, deeper and more timely and accurate information. This information would be password protected so that only real estate agents could gain access allowing them to remain in the preeminent position to serve their clients.

Simple enough in concept but it's clearly an enormous undertaking. So who would step up and pursue this strategy? The NAR appeared to be the best and maybe only suitable party to do so and they took on the challenge.

The development process began with a presentation by the NAR CEO Dale Stinton in May 2007 when he outlined the NAR's initiative to develop a Gateway or "Archive" of all the information available on all properties in the U.S.

From the beginning there was concern that this project was an attempt by the NAR to develop a nationwide MLS. This opinion was fueled as the individual selected by the NAR to present the project was from California where the State Realtors® Association had begun an initiative to build a statewide MLS.

Initial presentations were conceptual in nature with very few details concerning how the data would be gathered, who would do the actual acquisition, what would be the MLS's role in the project and when would the "Gateway," "Library" or "Archive" be available. At that time, there were no answers to these questions. In 2008 the NAR began assembling the staffing to tackle the project and by August of that year the Realtors® Property Resource (RPR) Advisory Board was appointed by then NAR President Dick Gaylord. Comprised of brokers, agents, MLS and association executives as well as several industry consultants, the first meeting was held in September. Dale Ross, a Realtor® from Maryland with a background in MLS operations, was selected as chair. The NAR selected Senior Vice President Bob Goldberg, also an individual with extensive real estate experience, having worked previously for PRC Realty Systems and on the development of Realtor.com, to lead the staff assembled for the project.

Even with the assembled talent on the RPR Advisory Board, the task to "build a nationwide archive of property records" was daunting. As with most projects of this magnitude, the Board formed separate work groups to address each component of the project. It authorized a 'work-for-hire' agreement with MOVE, Inc. to begin building a front end application for Realtors® use in accessing the database. At the same time, the Board was working on a business plan which included research on the long term viability for the RPR.

The largest challenge in developing the RPR was to identify, select and come to terms with a data provider that would be willing and able to provide the property record information to the RPR. The two largest providers of this information were First American and Fidelity Information Services. A 'Request For Proposal' (RFP) was prepared and sent to both firms. During this time, Fidelity went through several mergers and acquisitions. While First American declined to participate, Lender Processing Services, Inc. (LPS), was interested in partnering on the project. LPS also operated Cyberhomes (cyberhomes.com), which had developed a successful front end search program as well as an extensive reporting capability utilizing property record information.

The Board authorized Dale Ross to enter discussions with LPS regarding a partnership to build the RPR. At the same time, MOVE Inc. continued their contracted work and developed and initiated several successful beta tests with Realtor® Associations across the country.

The Board was advised that discussions with LPS were proceeding favorably and that a determination needed to be made regarding the direction that would be taken to build the RPR. As the "Proof of Concept" work with MOVE was wrapping up the decision was made to proceed with LPS.

And so RPR was officially announced in November 2009.

WHAT RPR IS AND ISN'T

The Realtors® Property Resource is one of the NAR's Second Century Initiatives and considered by Dale Stinton as the "ultimate" member benefit. RPR was created to provide single source, desktop access for public record information such as tax assessments, comparable data, liens, zoning, permits, environmental, neighborhoods,

school districts and community demographics. Its enhanced search features will allow in depth nationwide property searches as well as market-to-market comparisons and referral opportunities not currently available.

> **“** MLS and Realtor® Association Executives would be well advised to be reminded that Realtors® own the listing information, not the MLSs. **”**
>
> **WALT BACZKOWSKI**
> CEO, Metropolitan Consolidated Association of Realtors®

RPR will be a "living" database covering 147 million properties when it goes live in the second quarter of 2010. According to the NAR, RPR will include active and off-market listings licensed from the local MLSs but will go further, containing other important information using the "Wisdom of Realtor® Crowds" concept not generally found in MLS. The database will be national in scope and property information will never be purged. Rather than providing a three-year or five-year view of recent transactions the system will provide a 'real-time' growing archive or profile of information on every property in the U.S., regardless of whether a property has been involved in a recent transaction.

Contemplated data sets include but are not limited to:

- Listings (active and off-market) licensed from participating MLSs;

- Unlisted property information from homebuilders and FSBOs (aggregated using web-crawling technology and other means). This information will not be made available to the public;

- Public records;

- Parcel boundaries and mapping information;

- Mortgage and other lien information;

- Foreclosure information (e.g., notices of default and REOs);

- Archived properties' photos and other rich media;

Many think that the RPR announcement was done in haste and was rushed. Far from it. It was actually a series of

2005-2007

NOVEMBER 2005

Dale Stinton, who was the NAR's chief financial and chief information officer, took over the NAR reins as CEO.

MAY 2006

Marty Frame joined Fidelity National Real Estate Solutions (FNRES) as Chief Information Officer.

NOVEMBER 2006

FNRES launched Cyberhomes.

2008

JANUARY 2008

Second Century Ventures LLC, a new company was launched by the NAR to consider investments in the development of real estate technology applications.

MAY

The National Library/Archive was named "Gateway."

JULY

Realtors® Information Network, a wholly owned subsidiary of the NAR, signed an agreement with MOVE to build a front-end system proof of concept for the Gateway project and provide other related services.

Fidelity National Information Services Inc. (FNIS), a subsidiary of Fidelity National Financial (FNF), completed the spin-off of its mortgage processing services into a separate public company called Lender Processing Services Inc.

2009

JANUARY 2009

The NAR issued a Request For Proposal (RFP) to First American Financial (FAF) and FNF/FNIS/LPS to provide tax and other real estate data for the new "Realtors® Property Resource."

FEBRUARY

In conjunction with FNF's acquisition of LandAmerica, FNF sold off its interest in FNIS/Cyberhomes to LPS. LPS/Cyberhomes replied to the NAR RFP proposing wider alliances and more far reaching application of LPS assets and data.

MARCH

First American Financial (FAF) responded by indicating that they were not interested in pursuing the RFP.

JUNE

NAR/LPS reached an agreement in principle and began legal work on an agreement.

JULY

The Realtors® Information Network concluded its Gateway Project agreement ("work for hire") with MOVE under amicable conditions. The proof of concept received excellent reviews. The reason for selecting LPS/Cyberhomes was firstly that their frontend and reports were already integrated and in place and secondly, they already had the data needed.

Timeline

different developments that culminated in the formation of RPR. Here is a timeline of the key events that led up to the announcement in November 2009.

JULY 2007

Cyberhomes partnered with AOL.

MAY 2007

tinton outlined his 13 Second Century Initiatives with one of them being the stated goal of uilding a "Nationwide Archive of Property Records." The archive would include a real estate brary/archive online to provide Realtors® with data on every property in the U.S.

AUGUST

The NAR appointed the RPR Advisory Board to begin work on developing the nationwide property record database. The name Gateway was changed to Realtors® Property Resource (RPR) to better reflect the vision and the scope of the project.

OCTOBER 2008

Jay Gaskill, CEO of LPS Real Estate Group announced an impressive array of services including REO Market Analysis, Tax Servicing Solution and Neighborhood Outlook.

SEPTEMBER

The RPR Advisory Board was formed with 24 members including agents, brokers, MLS executives and association executives to determine how the RPR Project should be implemented; Dale Ross was appointed the first Chairman.

OCTOBER

The NAR and LPS concluded four months of negotiations and 16 agreements that included a 10-year agreement for LPS to provide the originally requested tax data, additional real estate data owned by LPS, a copy of the source code of Cyberhomes, hosting services and ongoing data aggregation, analytics and other services.

NOVEMBER 2009

At an official NAR webinar Stinton presented Beta versions of two far reaching Second Century Initiatives:
1. The NAR's new Consumer Facing Website of general real estate related information (HouseLogic) and…
2. The Realtors® Property Resource as a comprehensive online database of all properties in the U.S. as a Realtor® only membership benefit.

RPR Database Structure

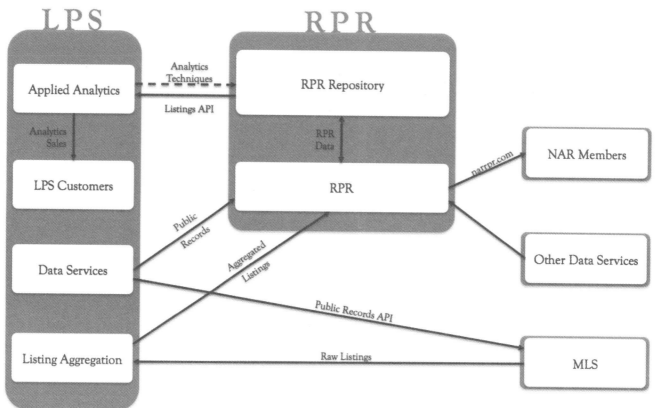

Source: NAR

- Environmental information;

- Disclosure documents (and any other transaction documents deemed suitable by a Realtor®);

- Insurance claims information;

- Community, school and demographic information;

- Property and community commentary provided by Realtors®;

- Property value estimates based on computer automated valuation models;

- Other sources of information as they become available.

There may be many other sets of information added to the database over time if those product sets are deemed desirable and make sense.

RPR will not be an MLS nor will it support offers of compensation and cooperation. The system will not

be designed as a marketplace and it will not support direct listing input (or the enforcement of MLS rules). It will be a private, password-protected system built for Realtors®, added to and edited by Realtors® and will not include a consumer-facing system. When finalized RPR will be an information reference, research and reporting system – the "Lexis-Nexis" of the real estate industry. Members will be able to access information provided by all participating brokers and MLSs (not just their own local MLS) along with the other broad categories of property-centric (rather than listing-centric) information.

Anything can change, but at this point in time, the NAR has stated that it is not the intent of the RPR to:

- Be or become a national MLS.

- Have anything to do with IDX.

- Carry any offers of cooperation and compensation.

- Carry any banner advertising.

AVMS AND RVMS

According to Wikipedia, real estate appraisal, property valuation or land valuation is the practice of developing an opinion of the value of real property. For the automation of that process we can thank Zillow for introducing the Automated Valuation Model (AVM) into mainstream real estate with the launch of their Zestimates in 2006. Initially ridiculed with huge margins of error, AVMs have become more accurate and are now offered by a large variety of companies.

AVMs were utilized extensively in the financial services industry in determining property values for mortgage loans as well as by Wall Street in determining the value for securitized loan packages. During the most recent financial crisis, sold property information alone proved to be inadequate as property values were declining at a pace not previously experienced. The values calculated by the AVMs did not in many cases, accurately predict market conditions. Today, although many banks and mortgage lenders use AVMs, they are more widely used to validate an appraisal.

> ❝ The future of MLS technology will be 'a la carte' choice. ❞

ROBERT BEMIS
CEO, Arizona Regional MLS, Inc.

In discussions with Fannie Mae, Freddie Mac and other Wall Street firms, RPR Chair Dale Ross inquired that should a valuation model be developed that included active real estate listing information coupled with the property sale data, would this have addressed the existing deficiency in the AVM and would they be interested in purchasing a product including this information. The representatives expressed extreme interest in such a product. This new product would provide the sustaining revenue

stream required to operate RPR, provide services to Realtors® at no cost and return the investment made by the NAR. It is the NAR's hope that the Realtor® Valuation Model (RVM) will become the "gold standard" utilized by the financial services industry at all levels.

> ❝ As an agent I feel like a "plankton" in the real estate pond's food chain. ❞

KRIS BERG
Broker, San Diego Castles Realty

It is important to note that the RVM does not yet exist, and although it will be initially based in large part on data provide by LPS, it will not be possible to operate effectively without the cooperation of the Brokerage community, and the involvement by state and local Realtor® Associations and the MLSs they operate.

Some say that the public record information coming from LPS does not universally meet local market requirements. In fact, according to David Charron, President and CEO of Metropolitan Regional Information Systems, Inc. (MRIS; mris.com), their data pales to what already exists in many markets. He expects LPS to invest mightily in acquiring more data from those MLSs that have already collected it.

Based on hallway chatter at the NAR Convention, comments such as "I am not giving my MLS information to them for free;" "The next step is a national MLS;" and "Let's see who else may be entering the market, maybe we will get a better deal" indicate that creating that "gold standard" will be a momentous task.

RPR CONCERNS

Everyone has been told that real estate data is extremely valuable but, as an industry, we have been struggling to find a way to maximize it. Here we are our own worst enemy. A survey conducted by the RPR found that 93% of the listings were found on multiple sites as agents compete to put them in as many places as possible. They seek no other compensation or reward other than to be 'found' on all these sites. MLS companies have been doing very well for quite some time now but there has also been a threat that this revenue stream may decline or even disappear.

When the NAR/RPR announced that they could earn millions of dollars — selling analytics from the combined MLS/tax data via the RVM model — and would not initially share the revenue with the MLSs or the brokers, until RPR began to breakeven, a huge controversy arose.

- Regardless what anyone says about the importance of creating the RPR, it is all about greed, says Charron. This is an initiative that started as a broker controlled revenue neutral entity. Upon further reflection, it was determined that it would be NAR owned and be a profit center. Currently RPR looks more like an agent centric initiative – something changed along the way.

> ❝ RPR will facilitate the notion and creation of a national MLS. This could be a great thing if the model for cooperation and compensation remains intact. ❞

DAVID CHARRON
CEO, MRIS

- RPR is rattling a lot of cages, says Brian Boero of 1000Watt Consulting. While this is largely a Realtor® family matter Boero says that one must immediately think of the impact it will have on companies such as Zillow that will see this as move onto their turf. But it's worth bearing in mind that Zillow's (and indeed most of the major online players') pitch to the industry is about delivering exposure and it will be hard for the NAR/RPR to be competitive with a Trulia or Zillow on things like SEO and PR.

> ❝ To what degree should brokers use the MLS data they have access to through the MLS? To the maximum benefit to themselves, over their competition... [W]ithin the law, MLS rules and Code of Ethics. ❞

SAUL KLEIN
CEO, Point2 Technologies

- Notorious R.O.B. believes the general mood of MLS operators ranges between hostility to cautious neutrality. The larger MLSs are biding their time to see what additional details will be released and what special offers may be extended to early adopters. Although R.O.B. publicly states that he thinks very highly of RPR he believes it will trigger a "civil war in the real estate industry" due to RPR's announcement not to initially share revenue.

- Brian Larson points out that there are many potential overlaps between a national property data site such as RPR and what Realtors® already get from their MLS. Some MLS operators think the NAR has no business creating the RPR and perceive it as the precursor to a national MLS — a cataclysmic prospect from their perspective.

- Clareity Consulting (callclareity.com) conducted a survey of MLS executives that attended the RPR webinar and the results were mixed. The most common question was: "What are the terms and details of the MLS data licensing agreement?" Several MLS executives planned to cooperate, some indicated they were cautiously undecided while others stated that they would not cooperate with RPR.

- Charron cautions MLSs to keep an open mind concerning the RPR. The interface is grand but the technology and impacts on local markets to adapt are untested. Regardless, MLSs and brokers should not roll over nor work exclusively with any entity; RPR included. They should not give up any revenues for local market "secret sauce." If there is money to be made on a national level the local market should participate as a total percentage of the revenues generated. According to Charron, RPR will furthermore facilitate the notion and creation of a national MLS. This could be a great thing if the model for cooperation and compensation remains intact. This model of course will likely continue to experience challenges and erosion going forward. It doesn't take much to leap ahead three to four years and wonder why the consumer would agree

and local Realtor® Associations and/or acquire each other so as to compete with the NAR/RPR.

MOVE, Inc.

When RIN/NAR terminated their agreement with MOVE (move.com), MOVE retained some of the intellectual property to the front-end they created for the NAR. MOVE is clearly a major player, whether managing the #1 consumer facing real estate portal (realtor.com) or potentially functioning as a national

> **❝** If we, as an Industry, are going to retain the "homeownership" space of the future, HouseLogic.com and RPR – a single-source national property database for Realtors®— are two significant stakes of declaration and determination. **❞**
>
>
> **TONI NELSON**
> Director of Strategic Initiatives, Prudential Gary Greene Realtors®

to pay a commission (certainly on the listing side). A national MLS will most assuredly facilitate this day of reckoning. Cannibalizing the base if done selectively, is a good thing if also done in concert with the local markets and the ones who stand to gain or lose (the brokers).

So what would it take for an MLS to participate in RPR? Here are four parts that Charron says he would expect to see:

- Broker concurrence and significant influence;

- Written guarantee that the RPR will not become an MLS;

- Restrictions on use of MLS data and derivative products;

- Revenue sharing with local markets.

COMPETITION

Below are some serious and significant players in the space that overlap with the new NAR/RPR/RVM initiatives. We fully expect that some of these companies will either form strong strategic alliances/partnerships with each other, state

MLS or a National Property Library/Archive. Watch closely as some changes are bound to happen here in 2010; they have had a longer warning/lead time than most players.

Zillow, Trulia, etc.

The major online real estate portals such as Zillow (zillow.com) and Trulia (trulia.com) and other consumer facing websites are already re-evaluating their current position and future strategies now that the NAR has entered the space. Although many are smaller than the NAR, they are more nimble than the NAR has traditionally been and with a strong entrepreneurial management style and years of experience, relationships and expertise in SEO, web traffic and public relations in this arena, the race is far from over. For example, Zillow could easy partner with First American and Trulia could easily be acquired by Google. Remember that although RPR has very broad usage rights of the public data licensed by LPS, no consumer facing usage is allowed so this part of the playing field is still wide open.

Google, Inc.

Certainly we can't ignore Google's (google.com) recent move of including a real estate overlay on Google Maps, which puts listings smack-dab in front of millions of Google users. It is very likely that few in the industry had any idea that the company spent the last several years quietly aggregating this content. Furthermore, Google also includes a unique page for every listing that incorporates photos, a map

> ❝ Whose ox gets gored, who benefits and where the money flows is anybody's guess at this point. But what I can safely say is that this is a significant shock to a system that needs it. ❞

BRIAN LARSON
Consultant and Lawyer

(including Street View), property details, directions, transit information and more; basically a listing detail page. No one knows what Google might do next.

LPS

LPS (lpssvcs.com) may sell RPR-derived products to the real estate industry as they still own Cyberhomes and may decide to continue to offer the service. Furthermore there is no exclusivity in the agreement between LPS and RPR and both parties may partner with others. That means LPS is not prohibited from working directly with MLSs or brokerages that opt out of working with RPR. This could be interesting.

First American Title

Remember the company that decided not to participate in the RFP? Well First American Financial (firstamericanfinancial.com) is LPS' main competitor and has the same, if not more, property data, tax data and excellent capabilities in data processing, data analytics and a history of institutional sales with government and financial institutions. One of the most well known and widely used is MarketLinx (marketlinx.com) and First American's Core Logic (corelogic.com) that provides free AVMs to MLSs

that share MLS data via its ValueMap product. Could they be a potential new partner for MOVE (they are both in Southern California) or maybe Zillow now that the NAR has picked LPS?

Others

Although not really competitors there are many other vendors that could enhance or compete with a national (or local) property database or consumer-facing website. All of them are open to offer their products and services to all companies, thereby making the race even more interesting.

For example, an excellent enhancement product is Home Junction, Inc. (homejunction.com) that will be releasing its SpatialMatch consumer-facing product sometime in the first quarter of 2010. This search engine will increase access to and control over the expanding data and research that consumers are demanding in the home search process. The company indicates that their data will be displayed geo-spatially and nearly 95 million houses will be included in the database, regardless of whether or not they are for sale.

Another possible competing product could be Vareti (vareti.com), that at the recent 2009 NAR trade exhibition announced that it would be offering "Property Valuations with a Competitive Edge," which it claims already includes content from local brokers in the top 100 markets covering 230 MLSs.

PROS AND CONS

To create a neutral list of pros and cons concerning RPR, we invited Gregg Larson and Matt Cohen of Clareity Consulting (callclareity.com) to give us their take as we wrapped up the writing of this trend early in December 2009. Here are their observations:

> *Pro:* RPR will provide extensive data resources to the Realtor® in one place, some of which is new like the Realtors® individual knowledge of each property, but some is data

MLSCloud

In the National Association of Realtors® *Profile of Home Sellers and Buyers*, MLS public websites are listed as the number one place consumers go to look for a home to purchase. The Houston Association of Realtors® (HAR), Metropolitan Regional Information Systems (MRIS), MLSListings.com, SoCal MLS, My Florida Homes MLS, MLS of Long Island (MLSLI) and others developed the idea for MLSCloud as a way of providing one easy place on the Internet for consumers to find those associations and MLSs that have consumer-facing sites.

What the experience and history of those associations has shown is that the more information you provide to consumers, the more informed they are. Seems simple, and it is. What some people expect is that those people will not then utilize the services of a Realtor®, but that has not proven to be the case. It has made the relationship between the client and Realtor® more efficient because clients come in already knowing what homes they want to visit, which significantly reduces the amount of time required to drive all over town looking for the home of their dreams.

Additionally, sellers have benefitted from MLS public Web sites like MLSCloud because they allow even more exposure for their listings, which hopefully sells their home faster and for closer to asking price. MLSCloud and other MLS public Web sites provide information to consumers, free leads to Realtor® and referrals to broker Web sites.

The MLSCloud homepage features a map with flags representing every MLS with a public Web site, and the sites may also be sorted by state to find them more easily. Any MLS may also have local market reports on MLSCloud, prepared courtesy of CAR and Clarus MarketMetrics®, which has been a great service to MLSs that did not have a statistics department or other easily produced market report.

In the first six months of its existence, MLSs and associations representing more than 600,000 Realtors® have links posted on MLSCloud. That is more than half of the entire NAR membership.

Con: Many MLSs may opt to provide very similar resources — if they don't already — to subscribers at minimal cost and without giving away any rights to use their data to a for-profit company. The individual MLSs are also not a single target with all the data for hackers or the DOJ.

Pro: The Realtor® Valuation Model may provide a "gold standard" AVM for other industries. The RPR Advisory Board has added Realtor® appraiser representation to the group to gain their important advice and point of view.

Con: There are plenty of AVMs available in an increasingly competitive and innovative marketplace. There is little barrier to entry for MLSs to use their own data to create enhanced AVMs or provide interpretive data around those AVMs. Until RPR overcomes what could be a significant MLS adoption threshold, it's unclear whether RPR can provide enough RVM coverage to provide an attractive offering for buyers needing national coverage to support the stated revenue projections and business model.

Pro: RPR will inspire many real estate software and information companies to innovate and provide new tools and resources similar to RPR's and embed them in MLS, broker and agent products.

Con: RPR's professional product offering may not be compelling enough for agents to leave the familiarity and convenience of their MLS or broker system.

that consumers already have access to and expect. RPR's resources include but are not limited to data such as demographics, school information, charts and other reports that assist in the interpretation of this data.

 TAKE AWAY

We have written about many trends the past 15 years. Most have materialized, undeniably slower than expected. A few faded and never really gained any real traction while some have become significant and have shaped our industry and created new companies that have gone on to become major national players. Just think, two decades ago we did not have email, online contracts, realtor.com, VOWs, IDX, a national profit sharing franchise or for that matter ActiveRain, EXIT, MOVE, Realogy, Zillow, zipRealty and many others. Well, add RPR to the list.

Sure, it could be gone in a couple of years; some pundits even said it was dead on arrival. Equally important are the many important questions that need to be answered such as:

- How will the Realtor®-only RPR allow MLSs to serve non-Realtors® — or will MLSs still need to license the data to serve those users?

- Will MLSs even be able to provide non-Realtor® listings data to the RPR?

- How will the site be monetized beyond selling the RVM to financial institutions and governmental agencies?

- Will RPR eventually sign non-compete agreements with existing MLSs?

- Will MLSs be able to enhance RPR data and relicense to produce revenue for the MLS?

- Will RPR provide a data-license agreement that MLSs will feel comfortable signing, as they do with any for-profit company, or will the majority of MLSs view RPR as their strategic partner?

All the above can be addressed and most likely will be.

What's different is that there is a real potential to develop the single best compilation of real estate data ever amalgamated and create a national standard with far reaching implications for financial services as well as Wall Street. But like everything else, this initiative — the Realtors® Property Resource — will only succeed with a consolidated and cooperative effort from everyone. If it does, it could very well prove to be the most significant undertaking in the history of organized real estate.

Book IV

Looking Back and Taking Stock
A Special 5th-Year Supplement

TREND SPOTTING 2006-2010

This is our 5th annual *Swanepoel TRENDS Report* and as we go to print the mortgage market is volatile, the housing market sliding, the real estate brokerage industry confused, technology is shaping productivity and the Internet is exploding. The game has changed dramatically.

When we published the first Report five years ago we did not expect it to become an annual Report, but clearly there was a need in the industry. The residential real estate brokerage industry was sitting right atop the vortex of all this change and in an industry short on quality and objective research the *Swanepoel TRENDS Report* was created to fill the void. Industry leaders, CEOs and Presidents, Association Executives, Brokers, Managers and Top Producing Agents all needed to be up-to-date with the trends, shifts and strategies that were shaping our industry.

Today, staying current with the trends is a vital requirement for any prudent and wise business person and entrepreneur, and with everyone busy and pressed for time the availability of a reliable, convenient source of information has become critical.

As we have said many times, we have no crystal ball and obviously cannot guarantee that any of the trends we identify will come to fruition. We do however invest hundreds and hundreds of hours into every *Swanepoel TRENDS Report* in an effort to provide quality, meaningful and objective information.

So with this our 5th edition of the *Swanepoel TRENDS Report* we thought it would be interesting to look back over the past few years and see how things panned out. We have categorized our past five year's Trends into the following categories for easy review:

- Real Estate Companies
- Outside Players
- Realtor® Associations
- Real Estate Data – Public and MLS
- The Consumer
- Globalization and Minorities
- Real Estate Business Models
- Knowledge, Skills and Professionalism
- Productivity and Profitability
- Technology
- The Internet
- Social Media

We hope you enjoy the journey back in time. We discovered many interesting things along the way.

Real Estate Companies

In December 05 we wrote about the "The Franchising Revival" (Trend #10) and affirmed that franchising was still one of the best opportunities for rapid expansion. We advised readers to expect more franchising options providing the traditional services and benefits, but cautioned that they would be packaged in different ways along with new alternatives.

In December 07 we discussed the "Clash of the Titans" (Trend #7) as we felt that the power brokers in the industry were flexing their muscles. Despite the downturn we suggested brokers and agents watch the following companies: EXIT, Home Services of America, Keller Williams Realty, Leading Real Estate Companies of the World, Long & Foster, NRT, Inc., Prudential, Realogy, RE/MAX and Weichert Realtors®. GMAC was listed as the most under utilized national brand and Real Living as the most promising new national brand.

Commentary

The battle for the top spots in market share and the number of agents has continued despite a downturn in the market. Understandably with the collapse of the housing market the majority of the large real estate brokerage companies and national franchises have contracted with many using the opportunity to close "poor" performing offices, acquire failing offices and consolidate market share.

But there were others like Keller Williams Realty that added thousands of agents over the past few years to become the 3rd largest real estate company in the country. HomeServices snagged Koenig & Strey when GMAC sold off its company owned stores. And GMAC (most under utilized brand) and Real Living (most promising brand) were acquired by Canada-based Brookfield Property Services and ended up consolidating under the Real Living brand.

Outside Players

In December 05 in "To Those Who Have … More Will Be Given" (Trend # 9) we forewarned that size, previously considered by many as more cost-prohibitive than effective, was no longer the case. We shared that a number of large players would most surely in the not too distant future dominate the lion's share of the market; some owned by incumbents and others by "outsiders." Possible entries were not only banks but also foreign corporations and Internet companies.

In December 06 we wrote about "The Entry of Outsiders" (Trend #4) and warned that as the industry continued its consolidation over the next few years, very large outsiders may be afforded an opportunity to enter and change the rules of the real estate transaction. Our best guess scenario was: Who — Priceline.com, Google, IAC, etc; When — no urgency, expect it to be gradual; How — the options are endless with purchase or partnering with an existing company the most likely.

Commentary

We saw fewer new "Outsiders" than expected. As a result of the mortgage crisis the most likely candidates (banks) were pre-occupied with survival and that significantly dampened their interest in the real estate brokerage industry. Also the general economic downturn encouraged other possible "Outsiders" like Home Depot to remain focused in their own niche.

However, newcomer and "Outsider" to the U.S. real estate industry, Canada's Brookfield Property Services, made headlines when it acquired the national GMAC Real Estate franchise and later Real Living; adding them both to its existing portfolio, Royal LePage. Together with Realogy and Cimmerman these three entities now collectively control 11 brands, including four Top 10 brands and seven Top 20 brands.

Realtor® Associations

In December 06 we urged action be taken under a trend titled "Extinction or Evolution" (Trend #9). We noted that the time had come for some serious introspection and action by Realtor® Associations. The NAR was alerted to huge MLS changes, emerging new business models and growing technology and the fact that business as usual would most certainly be a death notice. It was suggested that the NAR establish a very clear mission at all levels, retain competent leadership, become more open minded with respect to member needs and establish more appropriate member services through strategic alliances.

With enthusiasm we wrote in December 08 that "Organized Real Estate Moves" (Trend #4). The announcement of the NAR's second century initiatives could possibly be the change that will ensure its very survival. Underlying its objectives and perhaps the key to its future success will be finding the right strategic alliances to implement and manage the database, redefine and make the NAR's three-tiered structure more relevant and change the mind of the individual Realtor®.

Commentary

Well they did it. We are excited to report back that the NAR has taken a number of significant steps to evolve and grow instead of facing extinction. These are some of the boldest steps they have taken in its 101-year history.

See Trends #6 and #1 in this year's Report for the details.

Real Estate Data: Public and MLS

In December 05 we wrote about "Integrating and Managing the Real Estate Transaction" (Trend # 8). Title companies began to lead the way for a fully automated transaction with improvement in management platforms. Cost savings and efficiency through automation was promised. We did however warn not to expect an immediate perfect solution, rather the emergence of systems that would lead the industry toward a more seamless transaction.

In December 06 we advised that a "The Perfect Storm" (Trend #2) would lead to consolidation into larger MLSs and increased standardization within the process. We cautioned that it would not be easy or straightforward and that many sticky issues needed to be addressed before a national, quasi-public utility could become a reality; items such as data ownership, data security, data standardization, data integration, third party participation, etc. will be problematic.

In "Four Weddings and a Funeral" (Trend #4) in December 07 we advised that the borders and boundaries of MLS were changing as consolidation and collaboration gained momentum. The consumers' demand for information and the aggregation of listing information was pushing for the development of more public-facing websites. Add to that the interference of the federal government and it was clear that the management of real estate data was scheduled for a major overhaul.

In December 08 "The Boulevard of Broken Dreams" (Trend #5) affirmed the future of a national database and the consolidation of MLS'.

Commentary

Various MLSs have consolidated and many others are cooperating or sharing information. In November 2009 the NAR announced its Realtor® Property Resource (RPR), which according to Dale Stinton is the ultimate membership benefit.

See "Protect Your #1 Asset" (Trend #1) in this year's Swanepoel TRENDS Report for extensive discussion on this new initiative.

The Consumer

In December 05 we identified "A Population on the Move" (Trend #7). We explained that the potential geographical relocation of millions of baby boomers was in the initial stages as a result of growing unemployment and retirement. This shift was expected to have a national impact in redefining the makeup of many cities across the country; some areas exploding while others were experiencing an exodus.

In December 06 we chatted in Trend #6 about the "Young, Daring and Smart." They are very comfortable with the Internet, most have a page on MySpace and they have viewed countless video clips on YouTube. They have surfed, watched, recorded, listened and downloaded just about everything they can and now they are beginning to effect significant change in the real estate industry. Consumer and Realtor® demographics are being re-shaped by Generations X and Y and their presence will be felt more and more every year.

In December 07 "Gone in 60 Seconds" (Trend #6) recognized the threat of identity theft. In every corner of the business world today identity theft and poor data security run rampant and the real estate industry is finding that it isn't exempt. From the agents' desk to the company database customer confidentiality must be protected. While there is legislation at the federal and state levels that address the problem, brokers and agents were warned that any successful program must start at the local level and that failure to act will risk the loss of customer trust and confidence.

In December 08 we discussed "The Real Energy Crisis" (Trend #9). Oil impacts everything and everybody and in real estate it will shape housing values and future developments. We recommended that agents become more knowledgeable about energy conservation in order to assist homeowners in understanding all the significant new shifts in housing construction.

In December 08 green became "Winning the Gold" (Trend #8). We recommended that agents become much more involved in the exploding green movement in both residential and commercial real estate. Agents were also encouraged to ensure that they were well qualified by taking either the EcoBroker or the new NAR Green designation courses.

<u>*Commentary*</u>

This broad category illustrates the importance of consumers and how each year different issues emerge that have a direct impact on them. Collectively the past five years have shown us how important it is to stay in touch with the consumer, be it with their demographics, retirement and job seeking relocations, the shift towards the Internet and Social Media or the importance of their identities, green issues, etc.

All of these trends have and continue to be in play and are important examples like the people moving from states like Michigan and California to Arizona and Florida, the explosion of Facebook to 350 million people, the viewing of hundreds of millions of videos on You Tube and the almost daily reference to green initiatives or the fact that GREEN has become the NAR's fastest growing designation of all time. Tracking the changing needs and wants of the consumer has never been so important.

Globalization and Minorities

In December 05 Trend #6 described the "Impact of Immigrants and Minorities." The hunger for homeownership among the minority and foreign-born population segments will not only affect the market but also those who guide and direct it. Expect to see a significant number of real estate agents emerge from these segments. Look for promising opportunities to expand your ability to interact with the homebuyers in these various groups.

In December 06 we wrote about the "Tipping Point" (Trend #8). Globalization, immigration and a growing demand for U.S. real estate has created an industry tipping point. The immigrant and minority segments have a growing desire for homeownership and are moving to become a major part of the industry's future. Large U.S. franchises will continue to expand their brands internationally but there are also a number of international players that are poised to make a move into the U.S. market.

In December 07 we wrote about "Shattered Glass" (Trend #10). An increasingly large number of the leadership roles will be taken over by women, minority groups and the younger generation. The successful brokerage companies and associations will be those that embrace this monumental shift and prepare for the opportunity.

In December 08 we provided a different perspective in Trend #6 (The Foreign Factor) when we explained that globalization means more than just major U.S. real estate companies continuing to expand their brand internationally. We should expect new competition from non-U.S.–based companies that are also expanding. Examples to watch included Harcourts (New Zealand/Australia), Brookfield Residential Property Services (Canada) and Engel & Völkers (Germany).

Commentary

Casa Latino, a national franchise focusing on serving the Hispanic market, has enjoyed above average growth becoming one of the fastest growing real estate franchises in the country. Companies like RE/MAX surged abroad adding tens of new countries to their global portfolio while at the same time Germany-based Engel & Vöelkers expanded into Florida, the northeast and California. Although still very small, E&V has made more inroads into the U.S. than any other European company. Canada-based Brookfield burst onto the U.S. market with two major acquisitions during the past 15 months — GMAC and Real Living — making Brookfield now one of the top 10 players in North America.

In 2009 the NAR had its first African American president in its 100-year history, which was followed up with a woman sitting as president in 2010. We will surely have a Gen-X'er as NAR president this coming decade. Proxio created a new platform to enable the marketing of U.S. properties overseas (also headed up by a woman) while 30+ country real estate associations bandied together under the International Consortium of Real Estate Association (ICREA) to create WorldProperties.com.

Real Estate Business Models

In December 05 Trend #3 identified the growing "Proliferation of Business Models." Competition in the residential real estate brokerage industry is immense and intense. New business models are increasingly being created and existing models redefined. As franchising dominated the 70s, the 100% concept the 80s and technology the 90s, there is little doubt that something new will again cause a major shift in the industry.

In December 06 we wrote about "Paradigm Power" (Trend #1). There was an increasing proliferation and traction of new and existing real estate business models that was resulting in the creation of paradigm power. The traditional model can no longer remain unchanged if it hopes to survive the challenge of the new models that included: Residual Annuity, Discount, Auction, Multi-level Marketing, Fee For Service, etc. We also cautioned to watch those outsiders that receive cash from a Venture Capital company.

In December 07 we alerted to the "The Tug of War" taking place (Trend #7). A number of evolving and changing real estate business models were being offered but many brokers and agents ignored the change. Some models were offering potential buyers the option to view full, detailed "lead" information, the beginning of re-engineering the way agents relate to the consumer through the Internet.

Commentary

It's uncanny how four years later a book titled SHIFT identified the way to real estate profitability and cause a major shift as discussed in 2005. And the book was released by none other than Gary Keller of Keller Williams Realty. KW dates back to the 1980s and during the past few years it just exploded, and in

2009 surpassed RE/MAX to become the 3rd largest real estate company based on agent count. In so far as dominating business models, the first decade of the 21st Century can be labeled "Profit sharing."

There are many new business models like the online real estate brokerage company Redfin and the brand new bicycle group, Pedal Properties. There are relatively new business models that date back to the 1990s that have shown they can stand the test of time like ZipRealty and Assist-to-Sell, along with 30-year "old" returning brands with a complete new make-over like Better Homes and Gardens and Red Carpet Realty. Choices, confusion and the battle for market share are in full swing. You can read more about it in this year's Report in Trend #3.

Knowledge, Skills and Professionalism

In December 05 we wrote about "The Growing Knowledge and Skills Vacuum" (Trend #5). The dominance of "in-class" education would continue to lead the industry, but expect to see a growing number of brokers and agents gravitating toward an online approach to learning. Also expect a shift to more skills-based training as well as areas of specialization.

In December 06 we wrote about "The Swinging Door" (Trend #5). As a result of the market downturn several hundred thousand new licensees will leave the industry. For many the gravy train has come to an end and real estate professionals will have to accept that more of them will be fighting for fewer transactions; transactions carrying a lower commission. Professionals that are committed to being successful will have to take their career much more seriously.

In December 07 we wrote about "Thought Reform" (Trend #9). The backbone of the real estate industry — the agents — are regarded by the public as one of the least respected professions and by-and-large it's their own fault. Unfortunately the industry's answer has been to "tread water" and ignore the problem. To create a more professional real estate agent we must focus on creating an environment that will develop knowledgeable and more capable consultative, fee based, for-life relationship professionals.

In December 08 we warned agents in Trend #10 that "The Nightmare on Elm Street" could be the beginning of a disaster if they did not dot all the "i's" and cross all the "t's" on their Errors and Omissions insurance policies as there were a growing number of incidents where brokers failed to ensure their agents were covered for "prior acts." This sparked a new look into mandatory E&O coverage that currently exists in only 14 states.

Commentary

ARELLO tells us that the number of licensees has declined from a decade high of 2.79 million in 2007 to 2.43 million as we enter the next decade. Furthermore in a survey undertaken by the Chicago Association of Realtors® of their local associations it was reported that 69% of Realtors® had second jobs and only 27% of survey respondents listed real estate as their primary income. So, maybe not a swinging door but we definitely have many agents hiding behind the door.

Cengage Learning indicates that the whole fabric of real estate education is changing as the number of schools offering classroom courses is decreasing, resulting in a growing demand for online classes. The shift is bringing about an increase in the number of small companies offering continuing education courses; driving down the cost of online classes. RE BarCamp, an unconventional convention that 18 months ago did not exist is not drawing crowds every month in another city across the country. Many Realtors® are increasingly looking for knowledge and skill-based learning opportunities to help them address the needs of operating in today's new business and economic environment — unfortunately there are not enough quality courses or enough agents that seem to care to take the ones available.

Productivity and Profitability

In December 05 we discussed the "Rebirth of a New Middleman" (Trend #2). Numerous previous attempts to reduce the role of the real estate agent in the home selling and buying transaction were unsuccessful, but we cautioned brokers and agents not to think that this means it was over. Smart agents should hedge their bets by creating a balanced blending of business generated from both their own effort and that of a third-party. Success would however depend more upon the execution of a lead than on its generation.

In December 07 Trend #5 counseled agents to go "In Search of Productivity." We raised the alert of declining earnings and declining sales volume in the face of continued high agent counts. An overall decline in agent performance and productivity was imminent.

In December 08 we elevated this to Trend #1 when we itemized "Life After (During) a Down Market." Brokers need to shift their hiring priorities to quality versus quantity, improve their retention rates by focusing on mentoring and professional development and improve their margins with detailed business plans, ROI analysis and implementing new operational systems. Everyone that wants to succeed in the industry must re-structure and focus more on the consumer and the consumers' needs.

Commentary

Lead gen companies are still "fishing upstream" and offering extensive services although many national franchises and large brokerage companies have created their own lead generation systems. Technology is advancing daily, providing multiple avenues to the listing every day.

Agent productivity has dropped dramatically from around 13.5 transaction sides per agent at the height of the housing boom in 2005/6 to around 8.5 transaction sides per agent in 2009. Thousands of real estate brokerages have closed shop, hundreds of thousands of licensed agents have left the industry, yet a few companies are doing exceptionally well. You can succeed in a down market—just remain focused on the right things.

Technology

In December 05 Trend #1 titled, "Electronic Devices Take Center Stage," spoke about the growing importance of technology. We raised the alert concerning a much wider expansion of wireless networks, the shrinking of devices and the fact that they will become more powerful and provide and increasing selection of bundled services.

In December 06 we detailed "Web 2.0" (Trend #3). The Internet has become a collaborative source of information through instant voice, video or messaging; anywhere, anytime. Expect significant growth in mashups, RSS feeds, real-time collaboration, GPS systems, speech recognition, online valuations and vertical search. Expect the increasing proliferation of online listing information, more transparency, a continued shift of ad spending to the online medium and a further convergence of real estate technologies.

Commentary

There are many different technology innovations that underscore the electronic age we live in, perhaps none more so than the iPhone. Announced in January of 2007, the iPhone has become a global phenomena with 30 million sold within the first two years. Today there are also 100,000 different apps for the iPhone that have already created a $2.5 billion annual business.

With IDX "Houses for Sale" are now everywhere on the web; with AVM's many sites offering home valuations; and with RSS feeds everyone now has an abundance of content. Every day we hear about another acquisition, partnership, collaboration or convergence as more and more products and services become mainstream.

The Internet

In December 06 Trend #7 reported that "The Race is On." Google is expected to surpass Yahoo and grab the number 2 spot in web traffic, and in 2007 it will certainly take the lead over Microsoft to become the world's most visited site. In less than a decade an unknown brand has become one of the world's most recognized brands. This will apply equally in real estate where online brands with strong consumer appeal could become overnight sensations. Therefore traditional offline companies that want to remain successful will need to transfer their offline brand to the Internet.

In December 07 we counseled on "The New Digital Currency" (Trend #3). We detailed how listing and property information access and delivery methods have changed. The gate is open and the option to keep the information is slipping away. The opportunity for the industry, brokers and agents is to filter, process, deliver and interpret the information for the consumer; or someone else will.

In December 08 we identified in Trend #7 an increasing challenge with the "Information Highway Congestion." The information highway is clogged with too much traffic and has become a virtual parking lot. Successful brokers and agents must be aware that exponential growth in both the volume of information available and the methods for searching and retrieving that information has put the consumer on "overload" and they should position themselves as the "go to" person in each market.

Commentary

Well not only has Google become the #1 Search Engine, it has also become the "Microsoft" of the 21st Century and the most profitable Internet company of all time. Google is also in real estate in a big way by offering real estate overlay on Google Maps, a unique page for every real estate listing that incorporates photos, a map (including Street View), property details, directions, transit information and more.

It is estimated that there are about 1.7 billion people that use the Internet and that collectively there are least 20 billion web pages. Whether these numbers are right or not, all reports indicate a rapidly and continuously growing trend line. There is no question that the Internet has become a life changing phenomena.

Social Media

In December 06 we made readers aware of "Chasing The Consumer" irrespective of where they may be (Trend #4). As the availability of broadband continues to grow so will online video, making this potentially one of the strongest content-on-demand formats in the coming years. Social Media is expected to become the mainstream marketplace of the future. Agents are forewarned to keep their options open and their marketing diversified as evolution is in flux and few Social Medias will dominate for very long.

In December 07 we followed up by making "Two Worlds; One Industry" the #1 Trend. We drove the point home that online communities and social media networks were very important. The Internet has changed from browsing to searching and now it's all about sharing. The explosion of social networking in every facet of life has become staggering and is now entering real estate industry in a big way.

In December 08 we identified "The Power of One" (Trend #2). We illustrated how online tribes have now become the new power players. Social Media are evolving into platforms to provide quality content, advice and assistance to everyone. If used correctly Social Media will become the new engagement tool to earn respect and position the agent as the authority in a given area or field.

Commentary

Social Media exploded on the radar when Rupert Murdoch bought MySpace in 2006. It was however You Tube, Facebook and then Twitter that in the last two years have brought Social Media into the mainstream; forever changing media, the way we communicate, collaborate and market.

This market segment has become so large that beginning in 2010 the publishers of the Swanepoel TRENDS Report also now publish the Swanepoel SOCIAL Media Report. For an updated snapshot of the latest trends in Social Media read the Overview in the front of the Trends Report and for details on how to succeed in social media read the SOCIAL MEDIA Report.

References

Books, Magazines, Online News,
Presentations and Studies

10 Things to Know About Real Estate in 2010. Mullins, Luke, Luke. US News & World Report. December 21, 2009.

2008 Newspaper Section Readership Report. Newspaper Association of America. Fall 2007.

2009 Facebook and Twitter Growth by Age Group. Braziel, Lisa. Ignite Social Media. August 5, 2009.

2010 Home Price and Mortgage Rate Outlook: 5 Things to Know. Mullins, Luke. US News & World Report. June 17, 2009.

2010 Outlook - Local Interactive Advertising. Borrell Associates. October 19, 2009.

4 Ways to Build Your Brand, Business Using Flickr for Social Networking. Chorew, Amy. June 1, 2009.

74% of Americans Still Read Newspapers. Marketing Charts. November 19, 2009.

A Case Study on Survival in Real Estate. Frohriep, William Ph.D. March 2009.

A Conversation with Evan Williams. Oreilly Media. October 21, 2009.

A Fee-For-Service Future. Sparta, Kelle. Inman News. February 18, 2009.

A Pay-As-You-Go Real Estate Model. Kumar, Pooja. Inman News. February 1, 2009.

A Web of Housing Subsidies Threatens the Recovery. Lereah, David. December 10, 2009.

Adify Vertical Gauge Report. ADiFY. Second Quarter 2009.

Agent Ratings — To Play or Not to Play? Romito, Larry D. Quality Service Certification. Fourth Quarter 2009.

Agents Go to Town on Foreclosures, REOs. Inman News. June 4, 2009.

Agents Prepare for Tomorrow as Market Reveals Positive Signs. RISMedia. August 20, 2009.

Ailing Market Has Taken its Toll Not Only on Buyers and Sellers. Koeppel, David. MSN Money. 2009.

All Companies Engaging in Social Media Should Create Disclosure Policies for Employees and Agencies. MarketWire. October 6, 2009.

App Store Metrics. 148Apps.biz. December 22, 2009.

Are Fulltime Realtors® Turning Into Part-timers? Penza, Terese. North Shore – Barrington Association of Realtors®. November 4, 2009.

Are You Ready for the Next Generation of Real Estate? Chris, Sherry. Better Homes and Gardens Real Estate. May 5, 2009.

Auctions Today & Tomorrow. Varzos, Nicholas. Exclusively Auctions. November 2009.

Back From the Brink – Newspapers Stop Their Slide. Borrell Associates. August 4, 2009.

Banks Kick Commercial Real Estate Loans Down Road. Jonas, Llania. Reuters. July 23, 2009.

Beating the Recession. Ross, Bernice. Inman News. March 30, 2009.

Bernanke Says Commercial Property May Pose Risk for Economy. Lanman, Scott. Bloomberg. July 22, 2009.

Branding in the Social Age. Hahn, Robert. July 29, 2009.

Bridging the Generation Gap in the Workplace. Reyer, Liz. Reyer Coaching & Consulting. March 4, 2009.

Brokers Think Beyond the Cubicle. Umberger, Mary. Inman News. July 10, 2009.

California MLS off to Rocky Start. Carter, Matt. Inman News. September 2, 2009.

Camp Reinvent Launches Program to Help Real Estate Brokerages Reinvent Themselves. PCMS Consulting. September 3, 2009.

Capital Markets Showing Some Signs of Life. Auer, Tonie. Finance Lending. April 25, 2009.

Century 21 Launches Social Media Platform. REALTrends. April 29, 2009.

Century 21 Real Estate Recognized with Award for Effectiveness of Online Advertising Shift. Century 21 Real Estate. July 13, 2009.

Challenging Sales Market Will Push Default Rates Higher in 2009. Misonzhnik, Elaine. National Real Estate Investor. February 27, 2009.

Charge-Off And Delinquency Rates on Loans and Leases at Commercial Banks. Federal Reserve. Third Quarter 2009.

Cobroke Nation Asks, What Are You Showing Now? Inman News. April 8, 2009.

Code Name Waterfall: MOVE's Play for Active Rain. Carter, Matt, Inman News. March 4, 2009.

Coldwell Banker Boosts M&A in 08. Inman News. March 12, 2009.

Commercial Forecast – August 2009. National Association of Realtors®. August 2009.

Commercial Landlords Struggle to Refinance Loans. Levitt, David M. Bloomberg. January 15, 2009.

Commercial Loan Delinquencies to Rise, Barclays Says. Mulholland, Sarah. Bloomberg. December 3, 2009.

Commercial Market Trends. Drummond, Sara. CCIM Institute. First Quarter 2009.

Commercial Mortgage Delinquencies in US Rise to 11-Year High. Levitt, David M. Bloomberg. May 7, 2009.

Commercial Property Defaults Rise as Equity Dries Up. Levitt, David M. Bloomberg. April 2, 2009.

Commercial Property Prices in U.S. Fell 15% in 2008. Yu, Hui-Yong. Bloomberg. February 19, 2009.

Commercial Real Estate: Inside the Crisis. Veiga, Alex. Huffington Post. July 22, 2009.

Commercial Real Estate Drop Accelerates. Conrad, Katherine. San Jose Business Journal. July 22, 2009.

Commercial Real Estate Fundamentals Slip Sliding Away. Fleming, Sibley. National Real Estate Investor. May 27, 2009.

Commercial Real Estate Is a Time Bomb. Kopecki, Dawn. Bloomberg. July 9, 2009.

Commercial Real Estate Is the Next Shoe to Drop. Bell, Howard, Inman News. July 14, 2009.

Commercial Real Estate Woes Grow. Zibel, Alan. The Associated Press. July 9, 2009.

Commercial-Mortgage Crunch May Reach $1 Trillion. Mulholland, Sarah. Bloomberg. April 23, 2009.

Commissions Negotiable at Agent Invitation. Inman News. April 13, 2009.

Comparing Characteristics of Users of Newspaper Site, etc. Nielsen@Plan. Spring 2008.

Customize Your IDX Solution, Give Site Visitors the Information They Want. Aleagha, Peyman. May 25, 2009.

David Goliath Vie for Upper Hand. Carter, Matt Inman News. August 6, 2009.

Decline in Commercial Real Estate Sectors Appears to be Slowing. The Commercial Real Estate Outlook – National Association of Realtors®. August 19, 2009.

Did You Know 4.0. XPlane. The Economist. September 14, 2009.

Direct Mail Falls, E-Mail Soars. Borrell Associates. May 2009.

Direct Mail Goes Back to the Future. Carter, Matt. Inman News. September 10, 2009.

Disappearing Income. Armour, Stephanie. USA Today. December 2009.

Dos and Don'ts of Social Networking. Ross, Bernice. Inman News. May 4, 2009.

Doubling Down. Fleming, Sibley. November 13, 2009.

Dual Agent Survey. Downs, Ginger. Chicago Association of Realtors®. November 4, 2009.

Economic Downturn Pounds Commercial Real Estate Market. Kirchhoff, Sue. USA Today. January 12, 2009.

Economic Update – Fed Paying Attention to CRE Time Bomb. Stribling, Dees. July 23, 2009.

Economics of Search Marketing. Borrell Associates. June 11, 2009.

Economy Bottoming Out, Credit Remains Tight: Recovery Outlook Uncertain. CapLease. July 2009.

Economy Staggers Towards Uncertain Recovery as Banking, Credit and Real Estate Problems Persist. CapLease. October 2009.

Economy Watch – Case-Shiller Index Sees Another Uptick. Stribling, Dees. Finance Lending. August 26, 2009.

Edutizing. Wilson, Marilyn. WAV Group. July 2009.

Eight Ways to Profit as the U.S. Housing Recovery Gathers Steam. Spears, Larry D. Money Morning. December 2, 2009.

Engaging Users: User-Generated Content and Tools for Newspapers. Martire, Greg. Clark, Matire and Bartolomeo. June 2008.

Facebook is Leaving Twitter in the Dust, Says Hitwise. Cutler, Kim-Mai. DigitalBeat. October 29, 2009.

Facebook Visits Increased 194 Percent in Past Year. Experian Hitwise. October 9, 2009.

Falling Property Values, Mounting Pressures. Real Estate Investment Quarterly. Q4 2009.

FHA Changes Align Appraisal Rules. Carter, Matt. Inman News. September, 18, 2009.

Financial and Operational Analysis of Residential Brokerage Models. REALTrends. May 2009.

First-Time Homebuyer Tax Credit Is Fraudster's Delight. Indiviglio, Daniel. October 22, 2009.

First-Time Homebuyer Tax Credit. Christie, Les. CNNMoney. August 19, 2009.

First-Time Homebuyer Tax Credit. White, James R. U.S. Government Accountability Office. October 22, 2009.

FrontDoor to Push Listings to Newspapers. Inman News. August 3, 2009.

Future of Real Estate Makes Me Yelp. Bernheisel, Jeff. Inman News. August 28, 2009.

Gen Y Chooses Texting, Email Over SocNets. Marketing Charts. October 21, 2009.

Generation Y – An Opportunity and a Challenge. Jaffee, Glen. AlignMark, Inc. May 28, 2009.

GigaTweet – Counting the Number of Twitter Messages. Reed, Nathan. December 22, 2009.

Give Choice a Chance. Boles, Chuck. February 17, 2009.

Global MLS to Fill Several Voids. Kelly, Tom. Inman News. July 7, 2009.

GMAC Real Estate to Get New Name, CEO. Carter, Matt. Inman News. June 3, 2009

Google Builds Out a National Real Estate Search Engine. Magee, Matt. November 20, 2009

Google Continues to Feed the PubSubHubbub. Google Alerts Now In Real-Time. Siegler, MG. TechCrunch. August 19, 2009.

Has the Real Estate Market Bottomed? Zendrian, Alexandra. October 29, 2009

Homebuyer Tax Credit: Necessary or Evil? Olick, Diana. CNBC Real Estate. October 5, 2009.

Housing Industry Poised to Recover in 2010. Lereah, David. December 17, 2009.

Housing Market Trends & Outlook. Yun, Lawrence. National Association of Realtors®. December 9, 2009.

Housing Prices Forecast to Fall in 2010 – And Could Keep Falling for Years. Smith, Charles H. Economy. October 21, 2009.

Housing Slump May Worsen Next Year, Not Get Better. Bozzo, Albert. Investor's Guide to Real Estate. November 18, 2009.

How America Shops and Spends 2009. Newspaper Association of America. April 8, 2009.

How Big Is Google. Sorensen, Emma. Nielsen News Online. August 19, 2009.

How to Start Planning for Your Business 10, 20, or More Years Out. Kaucnik, Chris. Home Warranty of America. August 19, 2009.

IDC Finds More of the World's Population Connecting to the Internet in New Ways and Embracing Web 2.0 Activities. IDC. June 25, 2008.

IDX Debate: Is It Fair to Block Listings? Carter, Matt. Inman News. June 18, 2009.

IDX-If Real Estate Is Location, Location, Location – Then Map, Map, Map. Aleagha, Peyman. July 6, 2009.

iPhone App Store Statistics. MJelly. November 5, 2009.

Is Commercial Real Estate Really That Bad? Cullen, James. Daily Financial. July 23, 2009.

Is Facebook Today's MLS Book or are MLSs Tomorrow's Facebook? Wurzer, Michael. October 23, 2007.

Is It Time for You to Quit the Real Estate Business? Mantor, George W. The Associates Financial Group. May 11, 2009.

Is the Expanded Homebuyer Tax Credit Overkill? Lereah, David. November 24, 2009.

It's Time for MLS Consolidation. Inman News. June 11, 2009.

It's Time to Clobber Social Media (And Get Down to Business). Armano, David. Dachis Group. November 23, 2009.

It's Time to Take Up Tweeting. Ross Bernice. Inman News. March 2, 2009.

J.D. Power and Associates 2009 Home Buyer/Seller Study. J.D. Powers. June 2009.

John L. Scott Launches Social Network. Inman News. May 29, 2009.

Junk Fee or Necessity? Carter, Matt. Inman News. May 27, 2009.

Junk Fees Bad for Consumers. Inman News. June 24, 2009.

Keller Williams Climbs to Third Largest Real Estate Franchise. RISMedia. March 4, 2009.

Kill The Wasteful Homebuyer Tax Credit. Nutting, Mark. MarketWatch. November 12, 2009.

Losses on Commercial Real Estate Will Be Much, Much Worse Than Expected. Deutsche Bank. December 2009.

Magazine Ad Pages Decline Almost 26% in First Quarter. Clifford, Stephanie. April 15, 2009.

Main Street Goes Interactive. Borrell Associates. March 2009.

Many Would Shrug if Their Local Newspaper Closed. News Interest Index. March 12, 2009.

MBA Forecast for 2010; New Home Sales Up, Home Price Declines End. Norman, Dennis. Mortgage Bankers Association. October 16, 2009.

Micro-Blogging – How to Use Twitter for Market Alerts. Aleagha, Peyman. June 4, 2009.

Midyear Outlook … Tomorrow? Graziano, Anthony. CCIM Institute. 2009.

MLS 5 The MLS of the Future. Klein, Saul. Point2 Technologies. July 26, 2009.

MLS A View from Mars. 1000Watt Consulting. 2009.

MLS is More than Technology. Inman News. June 10, 2009.

MLS Must Admit Any Licensed Broker. Carter, Matt. Inman News. September 4, 2009.

MLS Usurping Brokers' Tech Role. Boardman, Teresa. Inman News. June 18, 2009.

MLSCloud Growing Fast. Inman News. September 3, 2009.

MLSCloud Looms Larger. Inman News. September 13, 2009.

Mobile Social Contextual Applications & Services. De Waele, Rudy. M-Trends.org April 24, 2009.

Mobile Social Hub - The Convergence of Mobile and Social Media for Businesses. Cooper, Jon. PhindMeMobile. November 8, 2009.

Mobile Social Networking Grows; Top 10 SocNets. Marketing Charts. November 17, 2009.

Mobilizing the Real Estate Office. Chan, Gilbert M. Inman News. March 9, 2009

Most Prestigious Occupations. Harris Poll. August 1, 2007.

Much Ado Over IDX Indexing. Boardman, Teresa. Inman News. May 21, 2009.

NAA 2007 Postal Survey Results. Newspaper Association of America. May 17, 2007.

NAR 2009 Member Profile. National Association of Realtors®. June 2009.

NAR Appoints Critic to MLS Committee. Carter, Matt. Inman News. May 28, 2008.

NAR Commercial Real Estate Index Shows Slowing Activity Expected in 2009. Kinchen, David M. Huntington News. November 22, 2009.

NAR Economic Research April 2009 Survey. National Association of Realtors®. April 2009.

NAR Invests in DocuSign. Inman News. November 16, 2009.

NAR Leadership Team White Paper. National Association of Realtors®. May 6, 2008.

NAR Leaps into the Fray in a Big Way. Inman News. November 9, 2009.

NAR Postpones Vote on Web Indexing. Carter, Matt. Inman News. May 19, 2009.

NAR to Launch New Info Site. REALTrends. November 10, 2009.

NAR to Revisit IDX Indexing Policy. Carter, Matt. Inman News. May 13, 2009.

New Brokerage Model. Davison, Marc. 1000Watt Consulting. June 30, 2009.

New Homebuyer Tax Credit Proposal: Impact on the Housing Market. Humphries, Stan. Zillow. November 5, 2009.

New MLS Service Catches Heat. Pisor, Erik. Inman News. August 25, 2009.

New National Real Estate Portal – PropertPurist. RealTrends. November 17, 2009.

New Views on Real Estate Compensation. Hurley, Buz; Kumar, Pooja; and Mohtes-Chan, Gilbert. February 12, 2009.

Newspaper Ad Revenue Could Fall as Much as 30%. Pérez-Peña, Richard. New York Times. April 15, 2009.

Newspaper Drives Online Traffic. Google. October 2007.

Newspaper's Real Estate Advertising Bubble to Burst. Mullman, Jeremy. March 5, 2009.

Newspapers Face a Challenging Calculus. Newspaper Association of America. February 26, 2009.

Next Generation Brokerage. Chris, Sherry. Better Homes and Gardens Real Estate. 2009.

No Recovery for US Property Markets until 2017. Jonas, Llania. Reuters. June 22, 2009.

No Time to Tweet? Tweetlater. Inman News. June 2, 2009.

On Google's Latest Real Estate Foray: Implications & Speculations. Buckley, Kathleen. 2009.

Online Advertising Through Social Media. Osborn, Alice. September 21, 2009.

Online Video Ad Budgets to Increase 50% in Next 12 Months? Rick, Christopher. September 9, 2009.

Outlook 2010. Thredgold, Jeff. Thredgold Economic Associates. December 2, 2009.

Planet Facebook – Is Social Networking Site a Phenomenon or a Fad? San Jose Mercury News. June 25, 2009.

Predictions 2010: Real Estate. Olick, Diana. CNBC. December 1, 2009.

Real Estate 2010 – Will It Be Better? Miller, Peter G. OurBroker.com. December 2009.

Real Estate Ad Spending Estimates. Borrell Associates. 2009.

Real Estate Agents Face a Shrinking Pie. Grigg, Dani. November 2, 2009.

Real Estate Brokerages Hit by Bankruptcy. Geffner, Marcie. Inman News. March 23, 2009.

Real Estate Marketing: Show vs. Tell. Hahn, Robert. June 16, 2009.

Real Estate Pros Go Moonlighting. Mattioli, Dana. Wall Street Journal. October 13, 2009.

Real Estate Recession Will Be Over in 2010. Woodard, Jim. Creators.com. 2009.

Real Estate Roundtable: CRE Challenges Far from Over. Heschmeyer, Mark. August 26, 2009.

Real Estate Tech for Non-Techies. Boardman, Teresa. Inman News. May 7, 2009.

Real Estate Without Walls. Mohtes-Chan, Gilbert, Roberts, Glenn Jr., Pisor, Erik, Keith, Natalie, Fooks, Bill,Kumar, Pooja, and Boardman, Teresa. March 12, 2009.

Realogy Haunted by Cendant's Past. Carter, Matt. Inman News. August 14, 2009.

Realogy Losses Narrow to $15 Million. Inman News. August 11, 2009.

Realogy Puts Homestore Behind It. Carter, Matt. Inman News. August 31, 2009.

Realogy Says Apollo Has Its Back. Carter, Matt. Inman News. February 26, 2009.

Realtor Association Launches Ratings Program. Inman News. April 21, 2009.

Realtor Bashing a Popular Pastime. Ross, Bernice. Inman News. May 18, 2009.

Realtors Repudiate Newspaper Ads. Newspaper Association of America. July 22, 2009.

Realtors® Property Resource: A Possible Business Model. Larson, Brian. October 6, 2009

Rebranding Real Estate. Berg, Kris. Inman News. June 10, 2009.

Recession is Easing, but Not Commercial Real Estate's Woes. Fleming, Sibley. August 12, 2009.

Recession Proof Franchise Attracting Brokers. Volkin, Michael. AreaPro Realty. March 18, 2009

Recession Reality: People with Good Jobs Need 2nd Jobs – Lawyers, Real Estate Agents, College Administrators All Looking for More Cash. Dorning, Anne-Marie. ABC News Internet Ventures. October 27, 2009.

Redfin Metro Brokers Stir Up Debate. Roberts, Glenn. Inman News. August 6, 2009.

Repositioning for the Future. Davison, Marc. 1000Watt Consulting. July 1, 2009.

Retail CAP Rates Shoot Through the Roof as Fundamentals Slide. Kalette, Denise. August 27, 2009.

RETechnology.com Announces Launch With MRIS and MRED. RISMedia. August 16, 2009.

Rising Commercial Delinquency Rates Could Set 13-Year Record. Kalette, Denise. National Real Estate Investor. February 5, 2009.

RPR Factsheet. National Association of Realtors®. November 5, 2009.

RPR Madness! NAR Unleashes National Property Database with Cyberhomes. Boero, Brian. November 7, 2009.
Say Goodbye to Newspaper Advertising. Carter, Matt. Inman News. August 6, 2009.

Shadow Inventory Rises 54 Percent. Cook, Steve. December 18, 2009.

Site Analytics: Facebook & Twitter. Compete.com. November 2009.

Six Social Media Trends for 2010. Armaro, David. Harvard Business Review. November 2, 2009.

Sizing Up Real Estate Politics. Berg, Kris. Inman News. August 26, 2009.

Soaring Home Sales Created a Stampede of New Real Estate Agents. Coombs, Joe. Washington Business Journal. May 23, 2008.

Social Media and Internet Trends for 2010. Ketsdever, Nathan. Compassion in Politics. September 8, 2009.

Social Media Epiphany. Davison, Marc. 1000Watt Consulting. June 10, 2009.

Social Media in 2010. Mayfield, Anthony. ICrossing. October 16, 2009.

Social Media Sites Don't Sell Real Estate. Boardman, Teresa. Inman News. April 9, 2009.

Social Media: Icing on the Cake. Berg, Kris. Inman News. April 29, 2009.

Social Networking and the New Real Estate Sphere of Influence. Aleagha, Peyman. February 23, 2009.

Social Networking's New Global Footprint. NielsenWire. March 9, 2009.

Social Networks – Not Just a Toy, but a Must Have Tool. Olling, Scott. May 13, 2009.

Social Networks Explode in Popularity. Consumer Internet Barometer. June 21, 2009.

Staying Strong – The 2009 Power Broker Report. Andre, Stephanie. RISMedia. April, 2009.

STUDY: Most Fortune 100 Companies Don't Get Twitter. Lavruskik, Vadim. Mashable. November 17, 2009.

TALF Program Expansion No Panacea for Commercial Real Estate. Fleming, Sibley. National Real Estate Investor. May 13, 2009.

Teaming Up for Real Estate Success. Keith, Natalie; Robinson, David; Rogers, Alison; and Wilkey, Marureen. Inman News. April 30, 2009.

Techie: Social Web Links Agents, Consumers. Inman News. May 14, 2009.

Ten Ways Newspapers are Preparing for Tomorrow. Goldstrom, Mort. Newspaper Association of America. December 2009.

Terms of Listing Syndication to Third Party Websites. Wav Group. November 2009.

The 500 Largest Brokers in the U.S. REALTrends. December 2009.

The Big Change in Real Estate. Hahn, Robert. 7DS Associates. August 12, 2009.

The Day the Newspaper Died. Dumpala, Preethi. July 4, 2009

The Factors that Contribute to the Survival of a Real Estate Sales Associate's Career: A Qualitative Study. Frohriep, William Ph.D. March 2, 2009.

The Need for Speed: The Importance of Next Generation Broadband Networks. Exell, Stephen; Atkinson, Rob; Ou, Daniel; and Castro, George. The Information Technology & Innovation Foundation. March 2009.

The Online Video Advertising Buyer's Guide. Web TV Enterprise (UK). September 2009.

The Real Estate Brokerage of the Future. Kreiser, Dale A. November 18, 2008.

The Recovery May Be Underway, But Feeling Safe Financially Will Take Longer. Revell, Janice. Money Magazine. November 10, 2009.

The Right Time for Bulk Buyers. Pisor, Erik. October 8, 2009.

The Rise of Media Mashups. Pisor, Erik. Inman News. May 11, 2009.

Three Ways to Measure Social Media. Dewald, Gahlord. Inman News. August 18, 2009.

Times Updates Social Media Guidelines. Standards and Practices Committee. Los Angeles Times. November 19, 2009.

Tools and Trends in Marketing Technology. Marketech. 2008.

Top 10 Must-Know Real Estate Trends for 2010. Petire, Shannon. FrontDoor.com. November 20, 2009.

Top 5 Web Trends of 2009. MacManus, Richard. ReadWriteWeb. September 7, 2009.

Top 6 Augmented Realty Mobile Apps. Parr, Ben. Mashable. August 19, 2009.

Trulia to Power Washington Postcom Search. Carter, Matt. Inman News. February 11, 2009.

Trust Can Mend Broker-Agent Relationship. Inman News. May 22, 2009.

Turnover – What Is It Costing You? Jaffee, Glenn. AlignMark, Inc. May 31, 2009.

TweetLister Releases Version 2. TweetLister.com. August 16, 2009.

Twitter Client Users. Berger, Michiel. Twitstat.com. December 22, 2009.

Twitter Tits 5 Billion Tweets. McCarthy, Caroline. CNET News. October 19, 2009.

U.S. Economy Forecast 2010, The Year of Severe Economic Contraction. Whitney, Mike. December 14, 2009.

U.S. Economy: The Big Questions for 2010. Englund, Michael. Action Economics. December 2009.

Under One Roof: Everyone Wins When Real Estate Brokerages and Banks Work Together. Bank of America. July 15, 2009.

Update: TC50: Facebook Is Cash-Flow Positive, Surpasses 300 Million Users. Cutler, Kim-Mai. DigitalBeat. September 15, 2009.

US Advertising Expenditures Declined 14.2% First Quarter 2009. TNS Media Intelligence. June 10, 2009.

VOWs Power to (Understand) the People. Roberts, Glenn. Inman News. August 10, 2009.

VOWs: MLS for the People. Inman News. March 26, 2009.

What Makes a Realtor Good: An Answer. Hahn, Robert. May 5, 2009.

What to Do about Web Advertising's Total Lack Of Recall? Burbank, John R. Nielsen News Online. January, 5, 2009.

When Gen-X Is in Charge – 5 Ways to Harness the Younger Leadership Style. Houlihan, Anne. Satori Seal. February 1, 2009.

Who Is Looking Online. Sorensen, Emma. Nielsen News Online. September 8, 2009.

Why Adults Have Fed Twitter's Growth. Miller, Claire Cain. New York Times. August 26, 2009.

Why Agent Selection Is Essential in Today's Market. Jaffee, Cabot L. AlignMark, Inc. May 23, 2009.

Why Are Newspapers Dying? Rogers, Tony. About.com. 2009.

Why Did Move Spurn ActiveRain? Carter, Matt. Inman News. March 6, 2009

Why This Bust Is Different. Der Hovanesian, Mara and Foust, Dean. BusinessWeek. November 16, 2009.

Why We Want a Faster Internet. Atkinson, Robert D. Information. 2009.

Widening Commercial RE Crisis Hits Banks. Eckblad, Marshall. Wall Street Journal. July 29, 2009.

Will It Be a Jobless Recovery for the US Economy Once Again? Valley, Matt. August 19, 2009.

Will the Dark Cloud of Commercial Real Estate Blot out the US Recovery? Patalon, William III. Money Morning.

World's Largest Real Estate Agents Switches Ad Budget from TV to Internet. Century 21. January 20, 2009.

Y,000,000,000uTube. Hurley, Chad. YouTube. October 9, 2009.

YouTube Lets Anyone Create Their Own iReport. Ostrow, Adam. Mashable. November 17, 2009.

Zillow.com and 180 Newspapers Launching Co-Branded Real Estate Websites. RISMedia. April 2, 2009.

ZipRealty Q1 Net Loss Totals $7,5 Million. Inman News. May 6, 2009

About The Author

Stefan Swanepoel is widely recognized as one the leading visionaries on real estate business trends, change and social media.

He has penned 15 books and reports including the best-seller Real Estate Confronts Reality, the highly acclaimed annual Swanepoel TRENDS Report and the new Swanepoel SOCIAL MEDIA Report.

Stefan has received numerous recognitions such as:

- Businessman of the Year (Jaycees)
- One of the Top 25 Technology Trainers in the US (Real Estate CyberSpace Society)
- One of the Top 100 Most Influential Real Estate Leaders in 2008 (Inman News)
- One of the Top 25 Most Connected Real Estate Professionals Online in 2009 (Proxio)
- One of the Top 50 People Who You Should Follow on Twitter in 2009 (Roost)

His academic accomplishments include a bachelor's in science, a master's in business economics and diplomas in arbitration, mergers and acquisitions, real estate, computer science and marketing.

Stefan writes and blogs throughout the year as events occur, new trends emerge, directions shift or new changes unfold. He is also the group organizer/coordinator for Real Estate Trends on all the leading social and business networks. You are invited to participate, join as a friend or group member, to any of the online services and to participate. For your easy reference here are the respective URL's:

 www.facebook.com/swanepoelinternational (Business, Real Estate & Social Media Trends)
www.facebook.com/swanepoel (Personal)

 www.linkedin.com/in/swanepoel

 www.twitter.com/swanepoel

Or you can find Stefan in any of the following communities:

 www.Activerain.com/groups/RealEstateTrends
www.Inman.com/Community/groups/Real-Estate-Trends
www.Realtown.com/Swanepoel/groups/Real-Estate-Trends
www.Brokeragentsocial.com/-trends
www.Realblogging.com/RealEstateTrends/
www.Trends.NewsGeni.us

Email him at Stefan@Swanepoel.com.

RealSure Consulting

stefan@realsure.com

tom@realsure.com

louis@realsure.com

tinus@realsure.com

dj@realsure.com

RealSure is a dynamic team of professionals ranging from experienced senior level executives (with over 100 years of combined real estate experience) to young Gen X/Y professionals.

Our consultants have been involved with some of the most significant projects that have impacted the real estate industry and have worked with many of the industry's largest companies during the last two decades.

The RealSure Team is qualified in multiple disciplines and well versed to assist your company — or Realtor® Association — in developing and implementing business solutions required to meet the challenges of this fast paced new economy.

Areas of expertise include:

Business Reengineering
Franchising Development
Strategic Brainstorming Sessions
International Business Expansion
Corporate Branding & Positioning
e-Business & Social Media Strategies
Development of Company/Association Business Plans

Call or email us to see how we may be able to assist you.

RealSure
CONSULTING

www.RealSure.com
California: (949) 954-7045 — Colorado: (970) 631-8240

RealSure Research & Publications

Reports

The *Swanepoel TRENDS Report* is the only report of its kind in the industry and the only collection that annualy details the top trends that are expected to impact the real estate business every year. The research covers all prominent news sources such as INMAN, REAL Trends,

| Swanepoel TRENDS (2010) | Swanepoel TRENDS (2009) | Swanepoel TRENDS (2008) | Swanepoel TRENDS (2007) | Swanepoel TRENDS (2006) |

RISMedia, Realty Times, Realtor® Magazine, NewsGeni.us and all most leading real estate blogs and social media networks such as ActiveRain, RealTown, BiggerPockets, Facebook and Twitter.

The *Swanepoel SOCIAL MEDIA Report* is a practical field guide on how to use Social Media effectively as a utility and tool for businesses. A special focus is given to the real estate industry.

Swanepoel
SOCIAL MEDIA
(2010)

Books & Whitepapers

Spanning a decade in the Real Estate Industry, the Real Estate Confront Series introduced through whitepapers and books, continued a discussion and evaluation of important and specific shifts that have impacted the Real Estate Industry.

Among the many timely topics covered are real estate commission structures, VOWs (Virtual Office Websites), real estate technology integration, telecommunications, online real estate education, the imvolvement by banks in real estate, goal setting & business planning, the bundling of services, profitability, the e-consumer and more.

| The Future (2003) | The e-Consumer (2000) | Reality (1997) |

| Information Explosion (2007) | Goal Setting & Business Planning (2006) | Bundled Services (2005) | Customer Acquisition (2004) | Profitability (2003) | The Banks (2001) | Technology (1999) |

Top ⑩ Trends

Transformational Change

BE AWARE. BE PREPARED. BE SUCCESSFUL.

Copies Item	Quantity Ordered	Unit Price	Shipping Per Unit	Total Price
1		$149.95	$9.95	
2-5		$129.95	$5.95	
6-10		$109.95	$5.95	
11-25		$99.95	$4.95	
26-50		$79.95	$3.95	
50+		$59.95	$2.95	

*Sales Tax Will be Added for California Orders

Total: _____

TO ORDER

Phone: (949) 954-7037
Online: www.RealEstateBooks.org
Mail: PO Box 7259
Laguna Niguel, CA 92607

Name (please print clearly)

_____

Address

_____

City   State   Zip

_____

Email   Telephone

Credit Card: AmEx ☐   Visa ☐   Mastercard ☐   Discover ☐

_____

Credit Card Number   Card Security Code (last 3 digit is located on the back of the card)

_____

Signature   Expiration Date

Social Media

A Field Guide for

Real Estate Professionals

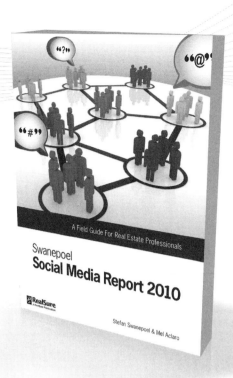

Swanepoel
Social Media Report 2010

RealSure

Stefan Swanepoel & Mel Aclaro

COPIES ITEM	QUANTITY ORDERED	UNIT PRICE	SHIPPING PER UNIT	TOTAL PRICE
1		$79.00	$9.95	
2-10		$68.05	$5.95	
11-25		$62.05	$4.95	
26-50		$52.05	$3.95	
50+		$43.05	$2.95	

Total: _____

*Sales Tax Will be Added for California Orders

TO ORDER

Phone: (949) 954-7037
Online: www.RealEstateBooks.org
Mail: PO Box 7259
Laguna Niguel, CA 92607

Name (please print clearly)
_____

Address
_____

_____

City _____ State _____ Zip _____

Email _____ Telephone _____

Credit Card: AmEx ☐   Visa ☐   Mastercard ☐   Discover ☐

Credit Card Number _____ Card Security Code (last 3 digit is located on the back of the card) _____

Signature _____ Expiration Date _____